PENGUIN BOOKS

THE BIRD OF MY LOVING

Mary Sheepshanks lives and works in Yorkshire. She has three children and a host of grandchildren – one of whom refers to her as his 'wild writing granny'.

She has also written three works of fiction, *A Price for Everything*, *Facing the Music* and her latest novel *Picking up the Pieces*, and two books of poetry, *Patterns in the Dark* and *Thinning Grapes*.

Chistmas '95

This Book
Belongs to

Maude Shewda

PRIMROSES and CATKINS © Gay Corran 1986

The Bird of My Loving

A Personal Response to Loss and Grief

Mary Sheepshanks

PENGUIN BOOKS

PENGUIN BOOKS

Published by the Penguin Group
Penguin Books Ltd, 27 Wrights Lane, London w8 5tz, England
Penguin Putnam Inc., 375 Hudson Street, New York, New York 10014, USA
Penguin Books Australia Ltd, Ringwood, Victoria, Australia
Penguin Books Canada Ltd, 10 Alcorn Avenue, Toronto, Ontario, Canada m4v 3b2
Penguin Books (NZ) Ltd, 182–190 Wairau Road, Auckland 10, New Zealand

Penguin Books Ltd, Registered Offices: Harmondsworth, Middlesex, England

First published by Michael Joseph 1997
Published in Penguin Books 1998
1 3 5 7 9 10 8 6 4 2

The poems 'The Bird of My Loving', 'At Needlepoint' and 'Winter' originally appeared in
Patterns in the Dark, published by the National Poetry Foundation, 1990; 'Clowning', 'Why
were You Born?', 'Borrowed Time', 'Cradle-song', 'Gateways' and 'Left-hand Gloves'
originally appeared in *Thinning Grapes*, published by the National Poetry Foundation, 1992.
The publishers and author gratefully acknowledge permission to quote 'The Voice' by
David Morgan Rees, copyright © David Morgan Rees, 1996.

Set in Monotype Baskerville
Printed in England by Clays Ltd, St Ives plc

He has achieved success who has lived well, laughed often and loved much; who has enjoyed the respect of intelligent men; who has filled his niche and accomplished his task; who has left the world better than he found it, whether by an improved poppy, a perfect poem or a rescued soul; who has never lacked appreciation of Earth's beauty or failed to express it; who has always looked for the best in others and given them the best he had; whose life was an inspiration; whose memory a benediction.

Bessie Anderson Stanley

Contents

Acknowledgements

Many people have helped me in the writing of this book and I am deeply grateful to them all. In order to preserve privacy, I have changed certain names.

To those friends who have been so generous in sharing their stories with me, but who do not wish to be identified by name, I owe a big debt. They will know who they are and their contributions have been invaluable.

I would like to give my special thanks and appreciation for their generosity and courage to Jane and Andrew Douglas-Home, Diana and Tim Hare, Juliet Ramsden, Elizabeth Ward and Jenni Napier – and, of course, to my own family, who, as always, have given me unstintingly of their love and strength. It was brave of my daughters and son to encourage me to attempt such a personal book.

I should like to thank Maggie Smith, counsellor and trainer, and all those from the caring and medical professions who gave me their viewpoints, and thank them especially for their tolerance in acting as sounding-boards for mine.

Without the encouragement and support of Susan Watt, my publisher and editor, this book would never have been written. I have been more touched than I can say by her faith in me.

Last, but by no means least, I would like to thank my agent Sarah Molloy for her friendship and endless patience.

The Bird of My Loving
(For Charlie)

To all the air I vainly cried:
'This octopus, possession, strangles me.
Can't I be loved and love
and still be free?'
But no one heard or listened
none replied,
until upon the green horizon of my view
you came to stand.

The bird of all my loving flew to you.

You held it for a moment
in your hand,
then opening up your fingers
to the sky, you said:
'Our love is liberty.
Feel free to fly
but know that I am true.'
Because you never tried
to pinion it
the bird of all my loving
stays with you.

Introduction

To write about bereavement is an awesome responsibility. It means dealing with acutely tender and private areas of people's memory: perhaps reopening wounds by knocking off scabs which may have only just started to heal over; it will mean reawakening emotions which have long been buried, and bringing old pain to the surface again. Perhaps it will mean talking about taboos.

When it was originally suggested to me that I might try to write this book, my first reaction was to say no. Who am I to dare add anything to what has already been written on the subject? My story is in no way unusual or remarkable; indeed, on the whole I think I have been luckier than most. But I have had my times of loss, sadness and anxiety and have been helped through them by books myself. During such bleak and bewildering periods I felt a hunger to know what other people's emotions were under similar circumstances; I wanted to know if there were other people out there, beyond my own personal acquaintances, who might have shared my feelings; to know whether my own reactions were normal or freakish.

I have been lucky in having wonderfully supportive family and friends, but alas this is not so for everyone. Reading the accounts of how other people have coped with their troubles can go some way towards helping. Each time we identify with the feelings or emotions expressed by someone else, it lessens, just a little, the awful isolation of grief. It is difficult to feel positive over the loss of someone greatly loved, over an apparent waste of life, a seemingly appalling injustice; we expend a lot of energy in grieving and perhaps one of the positive things it is possible to do with the pain of a harrowing experience is to share it, and share the things that helped us to survive.

For those dealing with the bereaved it might be useful also to read about what sort of reactions – or lack of them – have not been helpful. Friends and families of those in trouble long to know how other people have been helped to cope with disaster by those who love them and are part of their lives. We often ache to help but feel diffident about making an approach. If by sharing these thoughts I might help, to however small a degree, someone else's pain and bewilderment, then it must be worth trying.

Some of the feelings brought about by loss are truly commendable: courage, unselfishness, stoicism, compassion, loyalty. All these qualities can be brought out by the illness or death of someone we love, but we do not feel only such admirable emotions. Anger, fear, guilt, resentment, lethargy, self-pity, even feelings of madness – these are a common part of grief too, and are doubly painful because we feel not only ashamed of them but also contaminated by them. We have irrational thoughts. We become obsessed about things. We need to be reassured that we are not going dotty and are not sinful, because we are in the grip of feelings that are extremely powerful but seem unacceptable. They are a common part of grief.

Before I decided to try and accept the challenge to write this book, I asked each of my three grown-up children what they would feel about it. They all encouraged me to have a go.

'What if I say something you don't like?' I asked. 'Tell the story as I saw it, but not as you did? What if I embarrass you?' They all told me to tell my own truth, and I honour them for it. They have been my great delight and solace through rough times. Their support and laughter have always been only a telephone call away, and this goes for my sons-in-law and daughter-in-law too.

Some friends were more doubtful about the venture, worried perhaps that it might rekindle old pain for me, and set me back on my road to recovery. A few seemed shocked that I should even consider such a project, fearing that I might be guilty of committing that unacceptable lapse of taste in some British eyes – displaying private emotions in public. This book is not for them.

I have had to ask myself some uncomfortable questions about my own motives. Why *am* I writing this book? Is it in part a sort of exorcism process for myself, a personal therapy? Is it to some degree because I am flattered to have been asked? I find this hard to answer; these are not the motives I would like to own up to, and if I answered yes to both questions, it would certainly not represent my main reason or be the whole truth – but I suspect that, if I am totally honest, there must be an element of truth there too. I hope I am writing primarily for other bereaved people, especially those with less support than I have had, who need to be reassured that survival is not only desirable but – in time – actually possible.

I must emphasize that this book is a personal one and in no sense a 'how-to' textbook about what to do or what not to do. It tells my story, but also includes experiences and reactions which friends have been generous enough to share with me. Many of them have suffered far more than I have, and I can only salute their courage.

This book is really about life after death, not in the sense of a journey for an immortal soul – though I do personally believe in that – but about what it is like for those who are left waving on the platform. I hope this will not be read as a book of gloom and doom, but rather of encouragement and comfort.

There are no short cuts through this journey of grief; we have to walk every step of our own individual *via dolorosa*, and each will be different, but there are handy hints for travellers. There are lights along the way, even quite early on. Above all, there are many fellow travellers who have survived – and triumphed.

Clowning

Slap on white greasepaint
Pagliacci's disguise
To keep anguish hidden
From curious eyes.

Stick a joke in your hatband
Spray stars on your hair
Laughter's the clothing
To cover despair.

One dress to the cleaners
Sponge off any pain
Grief is like gravy
If spilt it can stain.

Prologue

I am lying on the top terrace outside my bedroom. I can smell the aromatic scent of the sun-baked Mediterranean herbs that grow up the hillside. I have never heard the crickets so loud before, but this is the middle of July, and we always used to come here in September. My battered Panama hat is tilted over my nose and I have kicked off my scruffy espadrilles. I have always loved the barefoot way of life.

Perched high above the sea, I am level with the topmost branches of ancient olive trees; their questioning silver fingers flutter against blue sky. I am asking questions too. I look back over the last few years and ask myself what stage I have reached in my new life. Have I finished my grieving process? Will I ever completely finish mourning? Do I want to?

It is very hot. A haze lies over arid, mysterious Albania, though it is not as mysterious as it used to be. You can visit it on a day trip now, and searchlights no longer scan the water at night for secret swimmers trying to cross over to Greece. A flotilla of small sailing boats has just disappeared from view, their pointed white sails like the wings of seagulls skimming close to the water. A big liner is passing, stately as a swan; its wash will soon reach our bay where my grandchildren, snorkelling round the rocks or floating on their Lilos will shriek with laughter. We wonder how long it will take them to stop screaming out, 'Look! There's a boat' every time one passes.

It is four years since Charlie died and the first time we have been back to Corfu.

I wondered how it would feel to return here after eight years. It brings back many memories: Charlie stamped his personality so strongly on anywhere he loved. We have not taken the same villa – that would have been too painful. He loved this island, though we only started coming after illness had already ruled out skiing, and it was always second-best to the mountains, which were his first love. But as usual, he was supremely adaptable. When one door closed for him, he opened a new one with relish and went forward. I must try to do the same.

The last holiday we all had together, before travelling became out of the question, was a bitter-sweet time and memories of that visit remind me painfully of the years when anxiety cast its long shadow over everything we did. I am glad to be free of that constant worry now.

Four years into widowhood, my life has undergone enormous changes and I am not the same person that I was. I have become more independent and self-reliant, but also more selfish. You get out of the habit of constantly considering someone else's wishes and needs, out of the habit of ministering. If I want to turn on my light and read in the night or listen to music, then I do so. No more tiptoeing down to the kitchen to make a silent cup of tea when I can't sleep – I have a kettle by my bed. If I want to go on working in the evening I do not have to break off to get dinner. If I choose to write until midnight and then eat cold baked beans out of the tin, there is no one to see.

I still miss Charlie, sometimes with a piercing stab of

longing that catches me unprepared, but for the most part it is now a background ache that I have got used to, and often hardly notice: it does not stop me enjoying myself. Though I sometimes long for someone to share things with, I doubt if I could ever again submerge my life in someone else's. When I see young lovers walking along entwined with each other, I feel nothing but joy for them: I too am lucky enough to have my green memories of love. But if I see middle-aged or elderly couples walking hand in hand, enjoying each other's company – wandering round gardens, going on holidays, *doing* things together – a shaft of pure envy sometimes goes through me, and I think fiercely how lovely it would be to have my life's companion still with me. I feel cheated of a fruitful time of autumnal sharing. I feel angry.

Then I remind myself how incredibly lucky I have been with my family, and in my life, and how very many people have never had half as many blessings as I have had. But this is a book about loss and coming to terms with one's feelings, and it would not be honest to pretend that envy does not occasionally creep in.

I miss the blending of two very different minds, the ability to amuse each other, the pillow-talk, the shared intimacy of discussing people or events. I still hate coming home alone, whether it be after I've done something interesting, or met someone new, or enjoyed a familiar pleasure – shared in the family life of my children and grandchildren perhaps – or stayed with close friends. I have got more used to this solo return, of course, and have to admit that there are also times when I am positively glad of my private space, grateful to get back to the comforting cosiness of my little house and the opportunity to be self-centred – but I can still be hit by a wave of emptiness.

In her autobiography, Joyce Grenfell quoted the heart-rending first letter home her small nephew had written to his mother from prep school: 'Everyone here goes around in twos. I go around in ones.' Those who have lost a beloved partner, be it through death or divorce, often feel like this.

'So how's My Love?' Charlie would always ask whenever I came in, whether it was after an absence of several days or merely from a routine trip to the supermarket. After he died one of our grandchildren said, 'I do miss Grandpa's big hello.' I do too.

In this beautiful setting, surrounded by those I love, it seems the ideal time and place to take stock of my life: to look back over my married years, from the early days when sorrow hit us so unexpectedly out of a clear sky, to the later years of Charlie's long illness and ultimate death. I need to review all that has happened to me since Charlie died, to face my hopes and fears for the future. It is a time for balancing priorities. Here, then, interwoven with the experiences of friends, is my story.

Later in the book, I have referred to the incident that triggered this poem. It was written in a moment of desolation after Charlie's death.

Dark Wind

I watched three mallard
ride a stallion wind, and go
careering up the dark November sky
with surging grace.

I envied them
and wished that I
could rise at such a pace
above my own black gusts of loneliness.

I wished that I could fly to you again
– to have you hold my hand
and touch my face,
your laughter blend with mine
as once it did
before a shroud of pain and illness
cloaked your light.

I long to feel
your presence blowing through
the echoing space
your loss has left in me.

I know I must release you
to explore eternity
– not clutch and cling –
but all the same
I fling my anguish on the storm
and shout your name aloud
to call you back,
searching the spaces in between
relentless clouds
for messages.

My cry is sucked up by the gale
and swallowed whole
– no flashing button
signals a reply

– I cannot find
an answering machine.

Part One

I was born at Eton, where my father was a master. My childhood bedroom looked out on one side across the water meadows of the Thames to a stunning view of Windsor Castle; from the other window we could see School Yard, with its statue of King Henry VI, the founder of Eton, and to the back of College chapel, where some twenty years later I was to be married. It would be hard to think of more romantic and historic views to feed the eye of an imaginative child.

Someone once told me that if you ask anyone what their first clear memory is, you learn a great deal about that person and their life. I am lucky with mine.

My first really vivid memory is of laughter: I am eighteen months old and we have just moved house. The new nursery seems enormous and my brother and I have been given yellow dusters to sit on and are helping the wonderfully named Mrs Merrydew polish the linoleum. She goes along first, on hands and knees, applying red Mansion Polish out of a round tin – I can smell it now – and we follow after her, paddling along on our bottoms and polishing for all our worth. We think it enormously funny and shriek with laughter. That particular film stops there – but the laughter has remained with me always, a spring which has never quite dried up even through times of awful drought.

Nowadays I think I would have been dubbed a wimp: I was one of those nervous, fearful children, who saw paper tigers under every tree. My father was always telling me not to cross my bridges until I came to them, but I was on a perpetual reconnaissance for danger. Later, life sent me some real tigers to deal with. I have learnt that one trip over an unsafe bridge is quite enough, and it is wiser to try to conserve energy for real disasters.

I had an unconventional education, and did not go to school till I was thirteen. My love of books and poetry was encouraged, but my education was very uneven, with big gaps in it; it was certainly not good training for disciplining the mind. All the same, it gave me some unusual experiences and has left me with many wonderful memories.

In 1953, I married Charles Sheepshanks, headmaster of a boy's preparatory school. I can't remember a first meeting with Charlie because our two families had always been close. Charlie sometimes came to spend part of his wartime leave with us at my grandparents' house in Wales. On one of these visits he said to me, 'When you grow up, I will take you to the ballet.' When I grew up, he did. I must have been about ten at the time of the original promise – he certainly didn't have marriage in mind then.

Charlie introduced me to skiing when I was eighteen and he invited me to join the party he and his uncle took to Switzerland each year. From the word go I absolutely adored it – skiing and music were perhaps the things we enjoyed sharing together most of all.

Though I had known Charlie all my life, I had certainly never viewed him in a romantic light. I thought he was one of the most amusing people I knew, wonderfully dashing and unconventional, even bordering on the eccentric. My brother,

David, and I had always loved his visits, but regarded him as my parents' friend. He was twenty years my senior and I thought he was frightfully old. I suppose it was on this skiing holiday together that he must have noticed that the little daughter of family friends had grown up, but I was absolutely stunned, about a year later, when he first proposed to me. He was very persistent, however, and it was a case of third time lucky.

It had to be the best decision of both our lives.

I think the parents of the boys at the school must have been appalled when Charlie produced this green girl as his wife, but they were very tolerant. I was less tolerant and found the early years of living in the school extremely difficult.

After we had been married for two years our first baby, Belinda, was born. Perhaps the birth of a child is the event that changes a woman more than anything else. Being in love can be a selfish process, but when you have a baby, you realize that for the first time you really do love someone much more than yourself. That's how it felt for me anyway. We were both enchanted with our little daughter.

Belinda was born in May. Two years later, a second baby was due, this time in October.

There were no anxieties about the birth. I had not been particularly well, but then I was not one of those women who bloom with pregnancy. I had very low blood pressure, as I had had the first time, and early on had picked up some sort of cystitis bug. For the last couple of months I had been plagued with persistent diarrhoea, which was boring and debilitating. Tests had been done, no conclusions reached, but no one seemed very bothered. It was thought to be due to swigging too much Bisodol for heartburn, or to an 'irritable bowel' – it certainly made me feel rather irritable, but it never crossed my mind for a moment that there might be anything wrong with the baby. Today's mothers are infinitely better informed than we were then, so many possible hazards are written about, so much more is discussed on television and in antenatal classes, that I don't think my generation had half the anxieties that can worry the modern parent. Whether it is a good thing to be so well prepared for all eventualities, I don't know.

When I went into labour unexpectedly early, I was upset to discover that Mr Fraser, my gynaecologist, in whom I had huge confidence, had gone away for a family funeral, and it was a strange doctor who delivered the baby, another little girl, early in the morning. I remember how he chatted and laughed with the nurses during the last stages of my labour about private jokes and things of mutual interest to them all, as if I were not there. I felt totally excluded – strange when I was the star performer in that particular drama. I had been given a shot of pethidine at some stage which didn't seem to do much for the pain but made me feel too woozy to get words out coherently. This experience gave me a useful glimpse into the frustration of feeling absolutely aware mentally, but unable to talk properly. I have sometimes cringed since, when unimaginative nurses or carers have spoken in front of stroke patients as if they were automatically dotty if they can't speak. How can we know? Years later, when my husband had a stroke and temporarily lost his power of speech, he confirmed for me afterwards how terrifying it was not to be able to speak, or even worse, to hear the wrong words coming out of one's mouth.

The birth itself was straightforward, if rather long, but, as the baby was born and the doctor held her up, I clearly remember noticing running sores on her legs. I had not minded at all which sex our first baby was, but I had very much wanted a boy this time, partly to satisfy my 'heir-conscious' parents and in-laws, and, to my shame, was disappointed to be told I had another daughter. The elation I had experienced when Belinda was born was completely missing and I felt like a stone. Belinda had been tiny but exceptionally pretty, a real pocket Venus, but I thought this baby was quite hideous. She weighed 5 lb, but as Belinda had weighed only just over that, this did not alarm me in any way. Nobody spoke to me much, and the strange feeling of being invisible at my own party continued. I now realize that no one knew what to say.

They did not give me the baby to hold for quite a time and then only for a brief moment when she was well wrapped up, explaining that premature babies were often blue, that it was nothing to worry about. When I asked about the sores on her legs, they said this was just due to being a bit early too. 'Prem babies often look a bit funny,' said the nurse, and whisked Amanda away. I accepted all this totally, although she wasn't *that* premature. I knew from my own mother that I had been three weeks early myself and, apart from causing inconvenience, there had been no problem.

In those days there was no question of fathers being present, so Charlie did not arrive till over an hour later. He rushed in armed with flowers and beaming. I pretended I was delighted with the baby, and would not admit to any disappointment over her sex, and if he felt any, he certainly did not show it. We decided to call her Amanda Rose.

The baby wasn't brought to me to feed till the following day: this proved very difficult and was also put down to her being premature, but I had recovered my equilibrium. I remember holding her against my cheek, telling her I was desperately sorry to have been so unwelcoming, that I didn't give a toss what sex she was, that I was thrilled with her and would love her to bits. Belinda was brought over to inspect her new sister.

Charlie and I joked that our baby would hardly win a beauty contest yet, but would probably stun us all in a few weeks' time. Feeding continued to be dreadfully difficult. I was discouraged from doing anything else for her – 'Still a bit too delicate' – and did not see her undressed. I was told her rather curious hands were again due to being premature, and would 'even out'. I don't remember feeling any doubts on this score.

When she was four days old, Mr Fraser returned. He was a dour Scot with a marvellous sense of humour and a tender heart under a gruff exterior, and we had become very fond of him during my first pregnancy, and he of us. He walked into my room looking particularly boot-faced, but I put this down to the black tie he was wearing out of respect for the dead relative, greeted him effusively and said proudly, 'Have you seen what I've done while you've been away? Aren't I clever?' He did not smile, he just walked over to the window and said, 'Has anyone said anything to you about the baby?'

I remember vividly the terrible lurch of the heart that his words gave me and, even more, the very unhappy look on his face. I asked if there was something wrong with Amanda. He said he was not happy about her and would like a paediatrician to check her out. I asked what was wrong but he said he didn't know. I asked if she was a spastic or a mongol – the only two conditions I had ever heard of. We didn't use the terms cerebral palsy and Down's syndrome then; I don't think I would have known what a syndrome was. Mr Fraser said he was sure it was neither of those conditions and in all his years had never seen a baby quite like her. She had, apparently, very small eyes, 'But, of course, she may just be a very small-eyed baby'; she probably had a heart defect, 'But surgeons can do brilliant things now'; her hands were slightly deformed and the running sores I had noticed as she was born were quite unusual. She didn't look 'right'.

I was devastated. I wished I had been told that there were problems straight away while I was feeling so numb and detached, but Mr Fraser explained that because I was his patient, and also because no one knew what was the matter with the baby, they had thought it better to wait till his return. He looked extremely upset and I thought it must be awful for him to have to walk in and burst this bombshell on me, a terribly hard thing for any doctor to do. He suggested I might like to ring Charlie and ask him to come straight over, but when I tried to telephone I simply couldn't speak, so he did it for me.

After the initial shock and disappointment, Charlie's greatest unhappiness was for me. From the start I think he felt it would be best if the baby died, and his feelings, though painful, were much more straightforward than mine. I veered between moments of wild, protective, love and horrendous feelings of revulsion and resentment, which shocked me to the core. I felt quite unable to tell anyone and was horrified that I could be like this – I thought it was wicked. If only someone could have told me, or I could have read in some book, that such feelings are common, what a comfort it would have been. I started to have nightmares in which either the baby turned into a monster or terrible monsters disconcertingly turned into babies. I would wake sweating and shaking, but again could not bring myself to tell anyone.

This primitive urge to reject the 'wrong' offspring is as strong in animals as the urge to succour the weakest one can be. I have watched with interest my dogs reacting in both ways over the years, though not simultaneously as we can do, and this frightful split in one's own reactions is deeply disturbing.

Mr Fraser called in a paediatrician, Dr Harris, who had a reputation as a brilliant diagnostician and a very clever man. I came to dread his visits. He was a dapper little man and, had he been an actor, I felt he would have been ideally cast in the role of Hercule Poirot. If I expected comfort or reassurance, I was soon to learn that sleuthing was the name of the game. I felt he regarded Amanda as a particularly challenging and exciting case, and that my role as her mother was not of the slightest interest to him. Poor Dr Harris – I know I shall paint a black picture of him, and I expect I am being unfair to him in many ways, but I can only tell the story from my point of view, and we looked at things through opposite ends of a telescope. No doubt he found me difficult too, frequently pestering him with questions and highly emotional. We certainly never dealt well with each other. I do know that he made some brilliant discoveries that have been of great use to medical science, and if our experiences helped in this way, then it gives a purpose to Amanda's short life, and one must be grateful to him for that.

We expect a lot of doctors. We expect them to be caring, understanding, compassionate and good communicators, as well as being clinically clever. The very best doctors – and there are many of them – are all these things, and then they are truly healers too. I am sure Dr Harris was clever, and no doubt his motives were impeccable, but it is in the nature of paediatrics that parents have to be dealt with as well as children, and I think anyone working in this field should acquire at least some basic understanding of a mother's feelings. Nowadays I know this is part of their training but, perhaps for some doctors, it is only possible to cope with the anguish with which they are so often confronted if they can detach themselves from it; but taken to extremes this is very chilling for the mother of a seriously sick child.

Twenty-five years later, I was again to be involved, through my eldest daughter, Belinda, with the agony of a child with a rare disability, and was again to be vividly aware of the enormous difference between being dealt with by those who could combine the sympathetic skills with the scientific ones and those who could not. It is hard to have confidence in someone with whom you feel you cannot communicate.

I would, of course, give anything to have Amanda whole, well and still with us, yet if I were offered my life over again and this was not to be, I would not choose to cut those six months out of it, because I learnt so much through them and they gave me so much more understanding of other people's troubles. Despite the pain, I now think it was an enriching experience, though naturally I didn't think this at the time.

Of course, I wanted answers to endless questions. What was her life expectancy? How handicapped would she be? Was this likely to include mental handicap too? Dr Harris called in an eye specialist who was as sensitive, understanding, and easy to talk to as I found Dr Harris difficult. Dr Harris seemed always to be whizzing in and out, snapping his black bag shut and arriving or departing without even a smile, no doubt running on a burning, investigative scent, like a terrier which is hot on the trail of a rabbit and temporarily deaf to all distracting calls or whistles. The eye specialist, also a busy man, sat on my bed and talked things through with us, explaining that we would have to wait for results of tests and might have to be very patient. He was also baffled by Amanda's condition and had not seen a baby quite like her either. He thought she might be blind, or at best have only very partial sight. Endless tests were done. Then Dr Harris said he wanted blood tests from me as well. He had a new idea, but would not discuss it. Why not?

I had been very spoilt by kind friends and parents of boys in the school when Belinda was born, and had revelled in all the congratulatory telegrams, flowers and letters that flooded in. Charlie had put the announcement of Amanda's birth in the papers the day after she was born, but things were very different now. I came to dread the sound of foot-steps stopping outside my door that might mean the arrival of joyful floral tributes. I prayed they would not be for me: they seemed a mockery. It was hard to know how to answer all the kind letters. In the end I hit on a formula and wrote: 'Unfortunately this little girl has not been given the good start in life that Belinda had, but we are still hoping things may improve.' I think Charlie fielded a good many telephone enquiries, and I received some touching and supportive letters.

A friend of my mother's wrote, saying, 'In the end, loving is so much better than being loved.' At the time this struck a resentful note in me, but of all those many kind letters this is the one that I can really remember. I couldn't get it out of my head. I wanted to love my baby, that went without saying, but I also passionately wanted her to be able to love me. This idea of one-way traffic is very hard to accept, particularly when one is young – but she was right. Now, much older, and perhaps a little wiser, I think I might rephrase the sentence, and say loving is not *better* but can be more *important* than being loved – but it is extremely difficult.

I asked Mr Fraser if he thought we should have the baby christened. He said he couldn't advise us from a religious point of view, but if it was something that mattered to us, then he thought we probably should. What I was really asking, as he well knew, was did he personally think the baby might suddenly die? His reaction gave me the answer. Charlie and I discussed it. We neither of us felt that, if Amanda were suddenly to go, it would make any difference to her reception by God, to her chances in heaven as it were, whether she were christened or not. If it did, then that was not a God or a faith I wanted to go on believing in. It was more a desperate desire to do what little we could for her, and do it right. When she was a week old we had a simple little service in my room, conducted by a friend who was a priest. Because I married so young I had hardly any close friends who had babies at that time. By a stroke of luck, one who did, Elizabeth, who had married Charlie's best man, had given birth to a daughter several days earlier in the same maternity home. I shall always be grateful to her for the support she gave me, and she stood as godmother to Amanda. I have never prayed more desperately for help and we were all four in tears. Afterwards Charlie said to me, 'You will never have to face anything as bad as that again.' He was wrong.

This was the year of the great Asian flu epidemic. Quite soon Charlie himself went down with it and became ill with pneumonia. Belinda was banned from being brought to see me in case she should carry infection.

My parents had been down to see us, and I, who spent

a lot of the time in or on the edge of tears, found myself completely unable to weep to my mother. I knew she longed, above all things, to take me in her arms and comfort me, to have me cry all over her, for her to be the one to mop me up as she had when I was little, but when she was with me my tap remained tightly turned off. I think she felt antagonistic to the baby because of what I was going through, and I don't blame her for this, though it made me very prickly and defensive. She did not want to hold Amanda. Years later she, who so adored babies and small children, found my handicapped grandson James just as difficult to cope with, and could never quite disguise her distaste, though she was full of concern for his parents. As it was, the moment she appeared, exuding love and anguish for me, I became brassy and brittle and held her off. I know it must have hurt her deeply, and to this day I regret it. I tried to explain and apologize but it made it worse. I ached for her and hated myself. I suppose I felt that if I once gave way to her passionate, overprotective love, from which, when I was growing up, I'd had such difficulty in fighting free, then I might go under and drown – and I was struggling to survive. I could cry to other people but not to my mother.

In some ways it was a relief when my parents returned to Wales, though with Charlie, the one person I wanted to have with me, unavailable, I felt very alone. When I rang home I was told that he was not well enough to speak to me. It was probably true; we didn't have a telephone in our bedroom, though there was one in our little sitting room next door, but I felt bitterly let down and resentful, however unfair this was.

I was greatly helped by one nurse in particular, a splendidly down-to-earth New Zealander with a sharp view of life and a pithy way with words. She frequently came to check up on me, usually managing to trump up some plausible excuse, but actually I knew just to help keep my spirits up. She was always ready to talk about Amanda in a frank and realistic way which I found enormously helpful. She also regaled me with hilarious stories about the other patients.

There were two mothers, sisters-in-law, who belonged to a famous circus family which was based locally, and they had just given birth to two walloping babies, each well over ten pounds, which, according to my nurse, made all the other babies in the maternity home look like puny little runts. One of these ladies was a trapeze artist and the other worked with animals and had gruesome scars all down her legs where she had once been savaged by a tiger. I used to take sneaky saunters down the passage during visiting hours to get a look at the fascinating circus folk who came to see them. Tremendously convivial and boozy parties went on in their rooms, and some of the other mothers complained about the noise, but I enjoyed eavesdropping on their riveting conversations far too much to mind.

It came as a complete revelation to me in the middle of great misery that the ordinary things that amuse us on a day-to-day basis don't cease to be funny. It is perfectly possible to laugh on one level while bleeding inside. In fact, grief, of which I had had no real previous personal experience, was very different from what I would have expected, had I given it any thought. It came as a surprise that it was not continuous, that there were moments which felt quite ordinary, and then, just when I was wondering if I was abnormal to be taking it so calmly – whoops! – a great tidal wave of misery would engulf me and I would feel I was drowning all over again.

In his book *A Grief Observed*, C. S. Lewis says, 'No one

ever told me that grief is so like fear.' He was so right. Grief is like a cuckoo's egg and mirrors many physical conditions, among them spells of terrible inertia and exhaustion – when it seems quite impossible to make even simple decisions, such as whether to get up and put another log on the fire, let alone make more complicated choices – and yet these bouts can be interspersed with almost frenetic bursts of activity. Freud said that grief mimics madness, which is certainly true, and yet there are times when one is surprised to find oneself not only functioning quite normally, but feeling normal too, and this immediately brings with it the guilty fear, 'Am I unnaturally hard-hearted? Why am I not hurting *now*?' And then it may suddenly be that the smallest thing, a twig rather than a branch, trips one up again and despair returns. When, years later, the husband of a friend of mine committed suicide, another widow who had walked the path of grief said to her, 'It won't hurt *all* the time.' I think one must accept these spells of anaesthesia with gratitude; they are normal and no doubt indispensable, but to those experiencing grief for the first time they can also be extremely disconcerting. Sleep-lessness is one of my own particular bugbears, but I have heard other people say that they just want to sleep all the time, that they are overcome by it.

Amanda, who had started out distinctly blue, became badly jaundiced and looked like a wizened little monkey. I alternated between thinking she was the ugliest baby I had ever seen and feeling a fierce, protective love that saw beauty in her tiny orange face. The eye of the beholder is all – my eye was unpredictable.

One day, when Amanda was about two weeks old, Dr Harris burst into my room looking extremely pleased. 'I have a diagnosis,' he announced excitedly. I had never seen him so animated. 'I know what's wrong with this baby.' My heart leapt. 'Are you going to be able to cure her?' I asked. He looked at me as if I was halfwitted. 'Oh, there's no question of a cure,' he said. 'The point is we now know what has caused the condition and what is wrong with her.' He had clearly done a brilliant bit of diagnosis, and had certainly worked extremely hard. I was told that very few paediatricians would have picked the condition up so fast, that he led the field in this research. Perhaps he felt congratulations were in order, but I was not in a celebratory mood. It was not what he had to tell me so much as the jubilant way in which he told it that was so hard for me to cope with.

I had picked up something called toxoplasmosis during my pregnancy and passed it on to the baby. It was then a new discovery. I was told there were only about ten recorded cases in the world, and therefore research was all very recent. Blindness and mental handicap were both thought to be among the effects; one child was known to have reached the age of two. There were probably lots of other cases which had never been recognized. It was a major breakthrough – but not for me and Amanda. I think the disease was then thought to be transmitted through pigs or cats. We had a dog but no cat, but we had stayed on a pig farm in Cornwall early in my pregnancy. Charlie's sister was married to a naval officer and at the time he was stationed at Plymouth and they had rented lodgings on a farm. We had gone down there for a week in April and I had been extremely unwell. In fact, I don't think the pig thing is mentioned nowadays, though I believe cats are. Anyway, at the time, this is how I imagined I must have picked it up.

I was longing to go home, but Amanda was not

considered well enough and influenza was still raging through the school. One day when I was feeding her, an agonizing performance because she had such difficulty sucking and tired so quickly, she suddenly started to haemorrhage from the mouth. Panic ensued. Dr Harris was sent for and she was given vitamin K injections. For the first time I remember voicing my uncertainties to him and asking, 'What is the point of all this resuscitation if she is so likely to die, and her quality of life would be so poor anyway?'

He gave me a good answer – the one really helpful thing he said to me, so I feel it is very important to record it. 'We do all we can for this baby's life,' he said. 'And if Nature then takes her and she dies, we know we have done what we can, and we live happily with that.' I didn't know about the happily bit, but I took his point, and was grateful for it. It helped me afterwards very much.

By this time, Amanda had been taken out of the nursery where the babies slept – the laudable fashion for keeping the baby at all times beside its mother had not yet come in – and she was put in a little side room, as I was told that her presence was upsetting to the other mothers. I can absolutely understand this now, but at the time it made me feel even more isolated, and very defensive on her behalf: she didn't look *that* bad. I was now looking after her as much as possible myself, but it was fraught with anxiety because one never knew what drama was going to happen next. Various doctors came in and out to see her, more I think for educational purposes than for her benefit. That is understandable, but to feel you have produced a fascinating freak is not conducive to joy and peace of mind.

Dr Harris would not commit himself about when or if she would be able to go home, and kept changing his mind.

He would announce that we could go out the next day, and then say no, we must stay at the nursing home a few more days. Back at home, Belinda was full of questions about her baby sister. We didn't know what line to take with her. Charlie was still ill. I existed in a funny kind of time bubble of my own: I could see the outside world going on but felt quite separate from it. The nightmares of monsters, and with them my private sense of guilt, persisted.

We had a wonderful GP, Duncan McNeill, who was the school doctor as well as our family doctor. An eccentric Scotsman, he was not everyone's pin-up medical practitioner, but he certainly was mine. For those he loved there was no limit to the amount of care and trouble he was prepared to bestow on his patients, and those he loved came from a wide cross-section of society. We both adored him but, being a man of strong and often unaccountable prejudices, he had his detractors. His passions were racing, ballet, gardening and his Pekingese dogs. Charlie shared the first three of these interests with him, but we all failed over the last one, as his dogs were unbelievably bad-tempered and we could none of us quite see the charm of being bitten to the bone by Snowy, chief Peke and most vicious snapper of them all, who had a snarl like a helicopter and a grip like a bulldog. There was also the Tiddler, the runt of a litter the McNeills had bred, whose legs were like flippers and who could only heave about on his stomach like a grounded seal. He was incontinent and rather smelly, but Duncan and his wife adored him.

We had several parents in the school who were connected with the racing world, many of whom were either old schoolfriends of Charlie's or had been with him in the war, and Duncan McNeill was always getting their sons out of school before important racing events on the flimsy pretext of inspecting their tonsils or athlete's foot, but actually to grill them for hot tips. These he would then generously pass on and, as he crammed his pork-pie hat on the back of his head, shrugged his long frame into his vast but threadbare camel-hair coat while stuffing his stethoscope into a pocket, and then lowered himself into his old green Jaguar car, he would lean out of the window to call out such vital instructions as, 'Put your last pair of knickers on Twinkletoes in the Two-Thirty.' He was also a brilliant doctor.

He and I shared a common misery in that we were both severe migraine sufferers, and he was always coming up with interesting new remedies, most of which were not in the text-books, one of the more novel being that it brought some relief if you lay with your head on a cushion in the plate-warming oven of a four-door Aga. As Duncan was six foot seven, this took up quite a lot of kitchen floor, and Agas are not always immediately available. I can't say I ever felt tempted to put this particular cure to the test, as the ovens in the school kitchen were gas, and for the headmaster's wife to be found with her head in one of them might have given the wrong impression.

Duncan McNeill made no secret of the fact that if he had delivered Amanda there would not have been so many early efforts at resuscitation. I'm sure he would not have taken steps to end her life, but neither would he have made such great efforts to prolong it. His views would not be acceptable today, and clearly his views on human babies and puppies did not coincide. From the beginning, he was convinced that Amanda's life span would be very limited and he was not at all keen on the idea of us having her home for what he felt would be a short and very traumatic time and one that would be deeply disturbing to Belinda. He may have been right – who can say? In the event it was not to happen. Nowadays far more advice would be available.

Eventually Dr Harris decreed that the moment really had come for us to go home. Amanda must have been over three weeks old and I couldn't go on staying in the nursing home indefinitely. Back at the school, Charlie was still in bed but convalescing, and my mother nobly came down from Wales to drive me and the baby home. We reactivated Belinda to the fact that her 'on/off' baby sister really was coming with me. Our nanny, Marian Stewart, who helped me with Belinda because I also worked in the school, got everything ready again for the arrival of a baby. Amanda was dressed and ready in her own carry-cot and I was sitting waiting with my coat on for my mother to arrive, when Dr Harris walked in. 'I've changed my mind,' he said. 'I'm taking Amanda into the children's wing of the hospital. You can go home, but I'll take the baby. We need to have her there for more tests.'

I was completely shattered. 'But I'm feeding her,' I protested. 'What shall I do?'

'Get Dr McNeill to give you stilboestrol injections to stop the milk. You can always come and give her a bottle in the hospital if you want to.' This most certainly would not have happened today, and a paediatrician who kindly read this section of the book was horrified by it.

I tried to explain how devastated I felt, how disappointed and upset I thought Belinda would be, and that I wanted so much to take the baby to her home, but he stopped me short.

'I'm afraid all that's not my problem,' he said. 'But the baby is my patient.'

I was not quick enough to say, 'No, the baby is your guinea-pig', and perhaps it was just as well. It represented my feelings, but he was doing what he thought was right. He took Amanda off with him there and then, saying I could go over to the hospital later.

This time, when my mother arrived to find me sitting alone with the suitcases, I had no trouble at all producing tears.

The next few months were a strange time. The jargon word 'bonding' had not come in, but from then on I felt as though Amanda and I sailed in different boats and that a terrifying but irresistible wind blew her little dinghy farther and farther out to sea, away from me, despite my desperate efforts to reverse this.

I drove the ten miles to the hospital every day to visit her, hoping to coincide with a time when I could give her a bottle so that I could at least do something for her. All the babies wore hospital garments, and her own clothes, in which she had arrived, were handed to me in a bag to take away. She was in a big and busy ward with some very sick babies, the majority of whom, I'm happy to say, usually got better and went home quite quickly, so I don't remember making more than passing relationships with other mothers. Most of the nursing staff were quite wonderful.

One day I arrived to find her cot empty, though her name was still on it. I turned cold and, after looking at all the babies in the ward, rushed to find a nurse.

'Oh, Mrs Sheepshanks, didn't they tell you? Your baby's already gone,' she said. I passed out. Poor girl, she was very distressed and it was in no way her fault. Dr Harris had taken Amanda with him to show medical students to whom he was lecturing, and the nurse not surprisingly thought he would have asked our permission, and that I knew. Writing this so many years later, I wondered if my feelings about this incident might have mellowed, but I still find it an inexcusable thing to have done and can feel my throat constrict as I think about it.

It was with no great feeling of confidence that we agreed to his request that Amanda should go up to the Hospital for Sick Children at Great Ormond Street for further opinions – but at least this time he asked us. Amanda was taken up to London by ambulance and I went up by train. It seems odd that I didn't travel with her, and I can't now remember why this was.

I had assumed that Charlie would automatically want to come too, and it came as a shock, and secretly a huge hurt, when he said he felt he could do nothing to help Amanda by coming and that, as he had already missed so much teaching through being ill, he did not feel he could take a day off. I longed to scream at him that I wanted him to be there just for me, but pride prevented me and I didn't. This seems very foolish to me now. I think we often make life unnecessarily difficult both for ourselves and for our nearest and dearest by not telling them what our needs are, and then being hurt when they don't perceive them. In the event, I can't have disguised my feelings as well as I thought I had because, about twenty minutes after I had arrived at the hospital and was waiting with Amanda, Charlie walked in, having driven up by car. This was a crucial point in our relationship, which had been starting to spiral downwards.

With hindsight and the experience of years, I can see that my total obsession with the baby must have been very hard for Charlie. Fathers can sometimes feel shut out by a wife's preoccupation with a new baby at the best of times, but when that child is extremely sick, the maternal instinct is activated to such a degree that it is hard for a woman to think of anything else. What spare energy I had was all given to Belinda, and Charlie, brilliant with small children but never good with babies anyway, must have felt as though his young wife had deserted him. For my part I felt – unfairly, of course – that because of his pneumonia, he had defected when I needed him most. I could probably talk of nothing else but Amanda, and he buried himself in school affairs. The fact that his place of work was also where we lived aggravated the problem considerably for us both.

I was inordinately pleased to see him at the hospital, and I think we both learnt something important from this incident.

From the moment we arrived at Great Ormond Street we were treated with the greatest kindness and understanding and felt very much included in every discussion. I held Amanda while she was examined by various doctors and though they were extremely interested in her, they never depersonalized the situation or made me feel that she was 'Exhibit A'. They could give us no more encouragement about the prognosis, but at least we felt we were fully in the picture and that nothing was being withheld from us. Dr Harris was given full credit for a brilliant diagnosis, but our difficulties and agonies as parents, and our concern for the effect on our other child, were part of the whole picture too. It can be done, and it made a huge difference to how we felt.

Afterwards Amanda returned to the local hospital, Charlie and I returned home to the school, and the routine of life, interrupted by daily visits to the children's ward, was resumed. I took up my work in the school again, and spent a lot of time with Belinda. Though I was extra grateful for her bright presence I found her lively company utterly exhausting and she, not surprisingly, became very demanding. Little children are quick to sense the tensions and miseries of grown-ups and no doubt pick up far more from unguarded conversations than we think they can understand.

Soon after this, Duncan McNeill, Mr Fraser and Charlie himself all started to put pressure on me – of the gentlest kind, but pressure all the same – not to go to the hospital every day. I suppose I was wearing myself out, and others saw more clearly than I did that there was no future in it. Doubtfully, I agreed to cut down my visits. I talked to the Sister of Amanda's ward, a lovely and wise woman, who suggested that I should miss a couple of days and see how that felt, and then perhaps come only three or four times a week. I missed my two days, guiltily conscious that it was a relief in many ways, but when I returned on the third day I was greeted by one of the young nurses – she can't have been more than eighteen – with scorn and hostility.

'Oh, you've bothered to come back, have you?' she asked. 'I thought you'd given up on your baby.' She can have had no idea what her words did to me.

In January Charlie and I went skiing. I felt dubious about leaving Amanda, but once we had left I have to say we had a wonderful week. Of course, there were moments of misery and anxiety, but they were not constant and it did us both good. We rediscovered the pleasure of each other's company. Belinda went to my parents, an arrangement that was lovely for all of them. I was incredibly lucky to have this support and help. Many people get no break from their burdens, and breaks can be like a drink in the desert.

There had been no change in Amanda while we were away. She had neither deteriorated seriously nor improved and though she frequently had respiratory infections, so far they had responded to antibiotics.

I was never to see any emotional response from her. She never smiled or appeared to give any sign of recognition. As far as I remember she didn't cry much either. I was always looking for signs of some reaction, making little tests – passing my hands in front of her eyes, talking to her, clapping my hands. It is hard to keep up a relationship when there is no response, especially if you are not doing the day-to-day caring either.

In February Dr Harris suddenly announced that they could no longer keep Amanda in the hospital. Up to that moment she had been there at his request; now, he said, we would have to make other arrangements. Though I was probably being unfair, it was hard to escape the feeling that, as far as research was concerned, she was of no more interest. We could take her to her own home or put her in a home for handicapped children. The choice was ours. It was here I found myself on shaky ground, and to this day I do not know what the right decision was. We discussed the pros and cons endlessly, and it was infinitely distressing.

Again this would be different today, and there would be much professional advice available to us. Some addresses are given at the back of this book. I am fairly sure that nowadays we would have had her home.

Duncan McNeill and Mr Fraser were both strongly of the opinion that we should not have her home. Charlie agreed with them, and though I think he tried to understand my doubts and difficulties and the torment these gave me, I felt as though everyone had ganged up against me.

We heard of a little nursing home on the south coast that specialized in caring for handicapped babies, and we went down to see it. Miss W, the woman who ran it, was exceptional – there is no other word for her. She was one of the loveliest people I have met. There were some heartbreaking children there – terribly severely handicapped – but all were beautifully looked after and treated with love and respect. It was her life's work. We spent a long time discussing things with her and she offered to take Amanda for as long or short a time as we wanted. We went home to think about it. We discussed it all the way home in the car and decided to give it a try. I told myself that she would have twenty-four-hour, trained nursing care, that it was just an interim decision, one that we could reverse at any moment, and that if things improved, we could change our minds, but I knew in my heart of hearts that we had taken a major step in a particular direction. There would certainly be no question of going down to see her several times a week.

Fashions in dealing with the difficulties of life vary, and there are many things that are looked at in a very different light now from how they were then, but there are no hard and fast rights and wrongs in this kind of situation, and one of the few things that makes me really angry is when people who have not experienced the torment of very controversial and delicate choices themselves see fit to cast judgement on other people's decisions. I only know that, many years later, my one lasting regret is that I feel I never had a proper chance to give Amanda the love that was in me to give to her while she lived, but this is a private and personal regret and I am not saying that it would necessarily have been best for everyone else concerned if we had played it differently. I'm not blaming anyone, even myself, for the decisions that we either accepted or took ourselves.

It was the beginning of March and Amanda was five months old when I went to collect her from the hospital to drive her down to Bognor. It was the first time since we had left the nursing home where she was born that I had been able to dress her in her own clothes and, as I did so, I could hardly see for tears. It seemed very bitter to me that I was collecting her only to abandon her again to someone else's care. My mother had come down to make the journey with me and if I had not had her with me, I don't think I could have carried it through and I might have bolted for home. We put Amanda in her carry-cot on the back seat of the car and set off for Sussex.

It was a nightmare journey.

The weather had started off grey and cold with showers of sleety rain but, as we progressed south, this unexpectedly turned to snow. I was terrified that if I had to stop, I might not be able to get going again, and the thought of being stuck in a snowstorm with this frail, sick little creature filled me with terror. Perhaps it was lucky that I had to concentrate so hard on the driving. We started to see other cars which had gone off the side of the road or got stuck. By the time we had been going two hours we were not half way. My mother thought we should turn back – which was very out of character – but I couldn't see that we would be any better off. We had to go up Goodwood Hill, a notoriously steep hill, and as we approached it there was an AA sign warning us that the road was closed. There were cars stuck all over the place and I didn't see where I could turn round. As we approached the hill, two AA patrol men on motor bikes appeared from nowhere. I shouted through the window that I had a sick baby on board and had to get to Bognor. 'Keep going,' they said and, one on each side of the car, they ran along, pushing for all they were worth. 'Don't stop, just keep steady, we'll get you up.' How we got up that hill I shall never know. I think those AA men were angels. I was the last car up the hill for several days, apparently. I couldn't even stop to thank them, though I wrote to the organization later. I do hope they passed my message on. Somehow we made it to Bognor. There was no question of driving home, the snow was far too thick and still falling. We had to abandon the car and take to the trains, which were still running, though much delayed. My farewell had to be very quick. Perhaps it was just as well. Lovely Miss W managed to get us a taxi to the station and pushed us into it, suggesting that I should wait three weeks before I visited. I was never to see Amanda again.

When we eventually got home, I felt punch-drunk. Charlie had made such a delicious but fearsome cocktail to revive us that quite soon my mother, for the first and only time in her life, actually was drunk. She sat on the sofa giggling helplessly and had to be helped to her feet before she could totter to the dining-room for some very essential food. I shall always be grateful to her for sharing that terrible day with me, and it went a long way to make up for my previous inability to unburden to her.

Four days later Charlie went down to collect the car. He went to see Amanda and reported that all was well. She appeared to have no ill effects from the journey and Miss W had got her checked out by their own doctor. Charlie did not tell me at the time that Miss W had told him that both she and the doctor felt that Amanda was unlikely to live for very long, though whether this was a question of weeks, months or even a little longer, they could not predict. It was more the informed guess – hunch if you like – of two people who had seen a lot of sick and handicapped babies. They would keep in touch with Dr Harris if there were unexpected problems. I rang up every few days. Amanda had got another chest infection and was back on antibiotics. I have little recollection of the days after I left Amanda at Bognor other than an overwhelming feeling of exhaustion and bleakness. I think I got on with my normal life, even though on one level I felt this was unnatural, but I felt hollow inside.

About three weeks later, I had a terrible and vivid nightmare. I dreamed that I was in a sort of cross between a museum and a laboratory. I knew it was a place where important research went on. It was quite interesting to start with and I wandered round looking at specimens of small reptiles preserved in jars and bottles. I was quite alone. Then suddenly I came across a glass jar which was much larger than the others. In it, pickled and perfectly preserved, was Amanda. I woke screaming the house down, and it was ages before Charlie could calm me down. I had a terrible sense of foreboding. The next day Miss W rang to say Amanda had died. Despite the dream, when the actual call came through, I was taken by surprise. I had convinced myself that if Amanda died, I would know the exact moment. I wished passionately that she had been at home, and was overwhelmed by the feeling that I had failed her by not being with her at the end.

Duncan McNeill, at our request, immediately rang Dr Harris to give him the news. A few hours later Charlie, looking very bothered, came to find me. I was lying on my bed feeling totally drained. Dr Harris had rung him to ask if they could have Amanda's body for research. It would mean delaying the funeral. (I am told this would be different now, and that in similar cases post-mortems can be arranged very speedily.) My immediate instinct was to say no, no, no, they can't have her. Hadn't they mucked her about enough already and done all their research while she was alive?

'I have said no, for the moment,' said Charlie. 'But I have also said I will talk to you. The decision must be yours. I will back you whatever you decide, but think about it.' In the end, of course, I said yes. What did it matter now, except that her life might be of use to some future mother and child? There wasn't really a choice.

My bachelor uncle-in-law was staying with us when the news came through. Charlie's father had died when he was two. Uncle Charles was like a father to Charlie and we were both devoted to him. He was much puzzled at my devastated reaction, and I remember him saying to me, 'But I thought you would be so relieved. I feel nothing but thankfulness for you both. How can you be so upset?' Of course relief was there on one level too, but how could I explain to this darling but bewildered bachelor about the intangible link between mother and child, or that I was grieving for might-have-beens? I am sure I was also having the physical reaction that comes after, not during, times of great stress.

On a brilliantly sunny day in April we drove down to Bognor for her funeral. There were only Charlie, me and kind Miss W present at the church. The little coffin was white and incredibly small. I had no idea what happened in a post-mortem, and I couldn't help wondering what Amanda's sad little body looked like now. The birds sang with heartless abandon, almond blossom and daffodils were out, the hedges had started to fuzz with green and there was no cloud in the sky. The snowy drive of a few weeks before seemed a million years ago, but this one is imprinted on my memory too.

*

Soon after this I had a useful experience. I was shopping in the village when I spied a girl I knew across the road – not a close friend, but someone whom I often met on the children's tea-party front.

I couldn't mistake her look of horror and panic as she saw me, and I watched her bolt for cover into the nearest shop. I felt winded with shock, but even at the time I did not blame her or feel angry: hurt and rebuffed, perhaps, but angry – no. I knew that a few months before, if our circumstances had been reversed, I might well have done exactly the same, not through lack of compassion but through a fear of not knowing what to do or say, a dread of making the wrong response. It was an invaluable lesson, because the only really wrong response is avoidance. I swore then that I would try not to run away from anyone else's unhappiness or trouble, even if the nuts and bolts of it should be outside my own experience.

People are afraid of the bereaved, afraid of upsetting them, of causing tears, of precipitating a display of emotion, but what does it matter if your sympathy makes someone weep? Tears are a useful outlet; it is what they are for. It is impossible always to say the right words, and what is helpful to one person may not be right for another, but I think a show of support is *always* right. You do not even have to speak: a touch on the arm, a quick hug, these can often get one's message of supportive concern through quicker and better than the most finely turned sentence. What is wrong with asking: 'What helps you most? Do you feel you want to talk about it?' These are questions that can be asked. Little practical things help – anything that eases life – because bereavement is exhausting and energy-consuming. Laughter, if appropriate, helps. As I had discovered, you do not suddenly lose your sense of humour because you are grieving. And, of course, there is time, the old enemy, but sometimes also the friend. You get over things because you have to; there is no choice.

I was to have one more encounter with Dr Harris. No one could tell us what the chances were of having another similarly affected baby because there was not yet enough information, but we were advised at any rate to wait for at least a year before we even thought about it. We didn't want Belinda to be an only child and, after waiting the suggested time, we decided to take the risk, with the rather precarious hope that lightning does not strike twice in the same place.

It seemed a long nine months but, just over two years after Amanda was born, Susannah Mary entered our lives and the birds sang for me again. There was no nonsense this time about minding what sex she was – I had only one question: 'Is she all right?'

'She looks perfectly normal to me, but we had better get Dr Harris to check her out tomorrow,' said Mr Fraser. I was immediately full of fears and suspicions. What were they hiding from me? I thought she looked perfectly normal too. In fact, I thought she was just about the most heavenly thing I'd ever seen, but for the next twenty-four hours I was on pins.

When Dr Harris came in, I felt myself go shaky inside with memories of many other visits and it was a terrific effort to try and give him a friendly greeting. My heart thumped, my hands went all sweaty and my voice almost disappeared. He gave Susannah a most thorough going-over and pronounced her healthy and normal in every way. Then I could have hugged him.

It would have been such an encouragement to me to know that even one mother had gone on to have a normal baby after giving birth to one with congenital toxoplasmosis, so I told him that if he ever had another patient in the same position I would go absolutely anywhere to talk to the mother and tell her about Susannah and give her hope.

I was very anxious to mend my fences with Dr Harris and end our relationship on a better note, aware that he had probably found me as difficult as I found him, and that by his own lights he had done his best for us, but his reply to my offer left me speechless.

'I shall be very lucky if I see another baby like Amanda in my lifetime,' said Dr Harris.

As I said, we looked at things from opposite points of view.

The loss of a child, at any age, is a very particular pain, and one that feels especially unnatural. I have written about my own loss of a baby, but by the time Amanda died I had already faced the fact that her life, had she lived, would not have been a normal one.

Here is a letter about a cot death. I think Jane Douglas-Home, who wrote it, expresses so well the pain, anger and bewilderment of such a tragedy, and also the sense of loss that women continue to feel about a baby for the rest of their lives. Again it is written from a woman's point of view, bravely touching on and acknowledging, but not exploring, the father's different outlook and the effect it had on him. It is courageous and generous of both husband and wife to allow this letter to be used. Because women are so physically linked to their babies, men can feel very isolated and left out of a woman's mourning. If a father had not particularly wanted that baby in the first place, he can be left with a burden of hidden and imagined guilt – not necessarily justifiable, of course. The guilt of the bereaved is a strange, irrational, private torment, and very common.

None of us is perfect in any circumstance or relationship. The loss of older children is a grief both parents share on equal terms, which is not to say that their way of expressing it or their emotional needs will be the same. The loss of a baby to a mother is acknowledged to be peculiarly physical as well as emotional. Nevertheless fathers can be affected physically too, and this story is yet another example of how, for all of us, health is bound up with mind, spirit and events.

Freddie was born on 13 December 1989. He weighed 8 lb 13 oz on arrival and appeared to be both beautiful and healthy. Having had two boys, Richard and Nicholas, I had thought a girl would be nice, but once Freddie arrived it could not have mattered less. Having been sick all through the pregnancy it was just wonderful to have the baby. Freddie had been my decision: Andrew did not want more children at that time, so the pregnancy was not as happy as it might have been for either of us.

The boys thought he was terrific. Andrew, who was very good with them, had never been great with small babies. Freddie was very much my baby, and I slept in his room. He was not a peaceful baby, and never slept for more than about three hours. On 27 January he woke early. I remember thinking I must soon put him on his back so that he could look at toys, and perhaps not want food and company quite so early. We had to go to a wedding that day, and K, who helped with the children, was coming to look after them. Freddie did not settle, so K took him for a walk. When she got back she said he had cried for ages, but was now asleep. I did think I might have picked him up sooner.

We lifted the pram into the house, and K took off his hat and gloves. She muttered that she was relieved when he made a noise because he hardly looked as if he was breathing. I went off for a couple of minutes and then came to say goodbye before going to the wedding.

Freddie's little hands were totally white and I thought it odd that he was cold. He was lying with his face down on the cot mattress, which was unusual, and as soon as I picked him up I knew there was something wrong – but I could not believe he was dead. I screamed to K and tried hopelessly to revive him. The hospital is only half a mile up the road and Andrew and I drove there as fast as possible. K had rung the doctors to warn them and they were waiting for us. They tried incredibly hard to resuscitate Freddie. They only stopped when I asked them to, because he would have been brain-damaged, having been starved of oxygen for so long. The doctor and nurse were shocked and upset too. It was a nightmare. I think I kept asking if he was dead. Eventually the doctor handed him back to me and said take him home. I couldn't imagine what I was going to do with him, but they said it was so that we could all say goodbye.

I took Freddie to his room and held on to him. I didn't want to put him down. I remember thinking he couldn't be dead and would wake up. I thought I ought to change his nappy but I could not bear to do it. Although I kissed and cuddled him I did not look at his eyes. It was like holding an empty shell. Freddie the person had gone. Andrew came to hold him, and both boys kissed him goodbye. Veronica, a great friend who was Freddie's godmother, came to support us and she held him. That was very touching – I'm not sure if I could have done the same.

Two uniformed police arrived soon after we got home. They were tactful and waited in the kitchen. As it was a 'sudden death' the CID had to come from Hawick. They seemed to take hours to get here. I can't remember if they asked me anything. I certainly never got the impression I was under suspicion, but was relieved I had not been on my own and there were witnesses to testify that I had not killed him. The police looked in his bedroom and at him. At some stage one of them told me I must put him in his cot rather than carry him around.

Finally the undertakers came. They only had an adult coffin and when I put Freddie in he looked so lost. I had wrapped him in a shawl, but by this time he was already cold and stiff. We watched the hearse take him away followed by a police car to escort him to Edinburgh for a post-mortem. Watching him go was unbelievable, yet there was nothing I could do.

I do not remember much about the rest of the day. That night I moved back into our bedroom for the first time since Freddie was born.

Organizing the funeral and all the technicalities was ghastly, but it did give us something to do. We wanted Freddie to be buried at Cornhill because the boys had been going to Sunday school there and we knew the vicar. However, Freddie had died in Scotland so that meant extra forms to fill in and journeys to Berwick, etc. A great friend helped me choose the flowers for the coffin and made sure they were where I wanted them. The funeral was supposedly private, but good friends turned up and also people from the village who I hardly knew and I was very touched. My brother drove all the way from Norfolk and back again that day. It was a pathetic little service with no hymns, but I can't remember anything except walking in holding Nicholas's hand with Richard in front with Andrew. While standing by the grave, Richard asked if he could see Freddie. Neither of the boys seemed to know what was going on, but I am glad they were there, even though my mother-in-law perhaps felt they should have been left at home. However, I had been excluded from my mother's funeral when I was five, and for a long time hoped her death was a lie and that she was still alive somewhere.

When the burial was over I thought, thank goodness I can go home and see Freddie now. Friends and family came back to lunch. It was all quite jolly and felt as if it were happening to someone else. I hated the idea that he died in January and would be so cold in his grave. It really upset me, though logically I knew it made no difference. Later, the four of us went back to the grave to see the flowers. So many people had sent them, it was really kind. I much preferred the ones that were sent to the funeral than the ones that came to the house – it was all too soon after the flowers I had received to celebrate his birth. One arrangement was identical to one I had received six weeks before – I nearly threw them out. One poor girl sent some beautiful freesias which were meant to be congratulations, but arrived a few days after he died. I know she was mortified.

The physical pain of grief surprised me. There seemed to be a hole in my chest as though a part of me had been torn out. My arms ached to hold him again. I was slightly comforted by the idea that I made a little home for him just above my left breast, and even though physically dead, he would live on in me.

Amongst the many letters we received was one from a woman we had never met. Her son, Rupert, had been a cot death seventeen years before and she wrote, saying that she still loved him as much now as when she had him. That idea seemed to make it less final, and I totally agree. I love Freddie as much now as when he died. He is still part of me and I think of him every day. Thinking of him like that helps with the fact that having lost a child you have lost not only the present but the future.

It is difficult to remember all the initial emotions. There was certainly anger. I was angry with Andrew for not having wanted and loved him like I did, and because our short time together was not the happiest – but Andrew kept his distance partly because there was a crisis at work and he was fantastically busy. I was angry with Freddie – how could he just give up and die. It was the time when there were all those Romanian orphans in the news – starving and uncared-for babies who had survived, and yet Freddie who was so loved had just decided life was not worth living. There was the feeling that it was not fair, as I had lost my mother so young, and my father was dead too: I had assumed that nothing could happen to my children because of this. Enormous pain and grief could suddenly hit me for no particular reason, or be set off by something obvious. There was anger and jealousy of all those women whose babies had survived. One of the worst times was when one of my greatest friends had her third child, a little girl, a few weeks later. I went to visit them, and held her, but I felt devastated and her mother knew how difficult it was. To this day I have not held another baby because I am terrified that if anything happened to the baby it would somehow be my fault.

People wrote wonderful letters. One person sent the words about the footprints in the sand and God carrying them in times of trouble. The idea is beautiful, but if anything, Freddie's death made me even less of a believer than before. I gained no comfort from religion whatsoever. After the funeral there was no contact from the vicar at all. I understand that this is the opposite in the Roman Catholic Church. Perhaps it would have been better.

I spoke a lot to Helen, a friend who had lost her little girl the year before. It was wonderful to talk to someone who had gone through all the emotions. The Cot-death Helpline were excellent, being strangers meant it was possible to say anything, including my negative thoughts. A part of me blamed myself, and felt perhaps I had not loved him enough or that I could have done something to prevent it happening. I suspect there will always be 'if onlys'.

Over the first months there was total exhaustion – even the

smallest things seemed incredibly difficult. Each night before going to sleep I would rerun the day Freddie died – as time went by I would include more details. Someone said that nature only lets you take in a little at a time. I think if reality had hit me all in one go it would have broken me. I grieved on my own, and definitely shut Andrew out. It was only when he became ill and over-stressed that we did talk about it, but possibly it was too late. Certainly Freddie's death had a huge effect on Andrew, although he has had difficulty admitting it. When Andrew first became ill, he denied that it had anything to do with it. When I went down with chronic active hepatitis, a disease of the immune system, I felt it must be linked to losing Freddie and the result of what grief had done to my body.

One of the things that helped me most was talking about Freddie and his death. My friends, without exception, listened uncomplainingly, which was – and is – wonderful. Even now I am grateful when someone mentions him. Veronica always remembers his birthday and the day he died. People gave us shrubs and trees in his memory. My sister-in-law Colette always has time to listen and comfort. It has been good remembering people's kindness. I do not see any sign of Richard and Nicholas being too affected by losing Freddie, and they mention him from time to time. They come with us to the grave on the anniversaries of his birth and death, but do not get upset.

After some months, Andrew and I discussed the possibility of having another baby. Andrew left the decision to me, but was supportive. I became pregnant immediately, but then miscarried at fifteen weeks, after going through the usual nausea. Losing that baby – another boy – was virtually painless compared to Freddie, and my main feeling was resignation that someone, somewhere felt two children was enough. It was after this that I got the hepatitis and had to go on steroids, which complicate pregnancy, so then I was sterilized. It was a relief as I could no longer dither about having babies, though there was a certain amount of pressure to have another to heal the pain. Perhaps it would have been easier.

Anne Diamond did wonders to publicize cot deaths and I am sure has saved many lives. When Freddie died, my mother-in-law had never heard of a cot death. However, when all the new theories are publicized it can be hard. The 'at risk' babies are those who were premature, small at birth, and born to smoking parents. Freddie was overdue by at least a week, weighed nearly nine pounds and neither Andrew nor I smoked. I still wonder why Freddie had to die and what I had done to deserve his death. The theory that only those who can cope are given trials makes me angry. You have to cope: there is no choice if you have a husband and other children. It sounds trite, but time was the greatest healer, and the only way to distance the pain.

I am not sure if Freddie's death changed me. It certainly did not make me a nicer person! I would like to think I am more understanding, but fear I am just less patient and more self-obsessed. Possibly I did learn what is important. One negative thing is that I am much more aware of what can go wrong – the thin line between life and death. Freddie's death was like turning off a light switch. I have lost the inner faith that things will go well, and am more fearful for my other children. I mind desperately about car seat-belts and any other danger areas.

I am not sure how much our marriage was affected. Neither of us is a great communicator, however, I think we are mainly at peace about Freddie now. It is pathetic he died so young, as Andrew would have loved him just like the others, given time. Our original disagreement about whether to have a third child has been a problem – a 'no-win' situation. We keep emotional distances, but probably would have done anyway.

Freddie would now be six, and it is odd to think how different our life would be. He only smiled at me once, that beautiful, radiant, wholehearted baby smile – I remember it so clearly, and the feeling and smell of him. I have kept the dress I was wearing when he died and it still has the milky stains on it. One comfort is that he did not suffer.

However painful Freddie's life and death were, given the choice I would go through it again. I have never, for one instant, regretted his short life.

After we moved to Yorkshire, Charlie and I watched with anguish and unbounded admiration while young neighbours of ours fought for, and then lost, an older child. Tim and Diana's little girl, Georgina, died when she was seven. They had lived with the shadow of the parting that was to come for most of that time.

Everyone in the village was rooting for Georgina, a gutsy, amusing, determined little girl whose huge personality was always far larger than her minute body. She herself hated being so tiny, and minded what she perceived as the indignity of her small frame. She couldn't know that though the space she occupied in a physical sense was minimal, the space she occupied in the minds and hearts of those who met her was enormous.

Tim and Diana's eldest child, Charlie, was a healthy four-year-old when Georgina was born. She was a very frail baby, who failed to thrive, but it took many investigations and she was a year old before cysteinosis, a rare defect of the kidneys, was diagnosed, and they realized how poor the prognosis was.

Di thinks her worst moments of blinding anger came then, on hearing the diagnosis, rather than when Georgina actually died. By that time they had not only faced the worst, but had watched her suffer too much to want to prolong her life. 'I felt so angry because I couldn't help my child,' she said to me. 'I felt I had failed her.' And she added, 'I think women are born being sorry about things which are not their fault.'

Tim was away in the Far East on business when Georgina's illness was diagnosed. When he came back his anger was initially directed towards the medical profession: 'If this doctor can't put her right, then we'll bloody well find one who can.' Like my own son-in-law, over his handicapped son, James, Tim eventually came to terms brilliantly with the dreadful disappointments and hurts, which were, to start with, such boulders in the path of the uncomplicated family life he had planned for and expected.

This early stage was also the one that put most strain on their marriage, while they both struggled in their different ways to come to terms with heartbreak. Later, as Georgina thrust herself into everyone's hearts and the whole family battled so valiantly to make the quality of her short life as good as possible, often in the face of awful sickness, they were remarkable for the support they gave each other, and that goes for their son, Charlie, too.

To look after a seriously sick child is a full-time career, but one that takes a terrible physical toll on a mother. Diana is both an asthmatic and a severe migraine sufferer herself – a willow wand who has bent double, but not broken, under fearful pressure. Those of us who watched from the side-lines could only marvel at her inner strength. One of the well-meaning but unhelpful things that was often said to her was, 'Isn't it lucky you're so strong?' Luck has nothing to do with it. During Charlie's long illness I remember being equally incensed when people said to me, 'Isn't it lucky you like nursing?' I don't. As Diana said to me, 'You do what you bloody have to, out of love – and because there isn't a choice.'

At some stage Tim and Diana took the knife-edge decision not to go for invasive treatment, but to follow the route of as much palliative care as possible. They have no regrets about this, and in their bereavement found comfort in feeling they had made the right choice. They had a very supportive paediatrician, who told them that he fully under-stood how they felt and, after they had made up their own minds, also told them that, given her particular circumstances, if Georgina had been his own daughter he would have made the same decision. They also had a wonderful GP – one of the three who helped me so much over Charlie's final illness too – who cared deeply about the whole family.

Tim and Diana were determined that Georgina, within her narrow physical limits, should lead as normal a life as possible. She was very bright, but the first school they sent her to was extraordinarily unhelpful about her condition and allowed her no quarter whatsoever, and they had to take her away. Then they found a wonderful village school nearby whose whole attitude was completely different. After Geor-gina died, Tim and Diana raised the money for a memorial library for this school.

Diana says, looking back on those seven years, that she learnt to be a wonderful actress and put on a bright show when she was often falling apart inside. Six months before Georgina died, they had a family holiday in the States and took the children to Disneyland. Georgina adored it. The final decline, when it came, was exacerbated by shingles. After many false alarms over the years, they knew the last six weeks of her life were the final ones. Like me with Charlie, Diana had envisaged that the actual moments of death would be easy, but it was horrendous. 'Now when I see in any death announcement the word "peacefully" I wonder if it was really so,' said Diana.

I shall never forget Georgina's funeral. Not long before, purely out of duty, I had attended, in the same church, the funeral of a singularly disagreeable old man. He was not without talent, but had never used his gifts and was a byword locally as a malevolent old misery-guts. You could have counted the congregation on two hands. I was pierced by the sadness of an apparently wasted life and the unmourned departure of a human being. At Georgina's service the church was full to overflowing.

After Georgina's death, Diana describes existence as 'real "north face of the Eiger stuff" – one small precarious toehold after another, a step at a time and don't look down.' She remembers feeling like an empty vessel, a zombie, and being terrified that her brain would never function properly again. 'I used to feel that Georgina had taken all that was best in me with her.'

Sometimes it would have been easy just to give up. Often it would have been easier to stay in bed all day. She made a rule for herself that she would be up, dressed, and with make-up on by 8.15 each morning. Tim and Charlie kept her going. She describes how redundant she felt after giving so much of her time and energy to her child, 'like suddenly being fired from a top job.' Tim told me how much easier he felt it was for him to go off to work and escape into that, whereas Diana's work had been in the home, centred round Georgina, and all the reminders of her were still constantly there.

A friend gave the Hares a book by Ranulph Fiennes,

the explorer, and wrote in it, 'For Tim and Di – who have a different kind of courage.' How right they were.

After Georgina died Diana met a friend at a party whom they had not seen for some time. He greeted her enthusiastically and said all the usual social things, like 'Lovely to see you' and 'How are you all?' Thinking he probably didn't know about their tragedy and might be mortified if he discovered afterwards, she said, 'Well, we're doing all right, as well as can be expected. But did you know we'd lost Georgina?' To which, looking desperately round for a quick escape, he answered, 'Yes I did know actually – but we don't want to get maudlin, do we?' A breathtaking example of how not to treat the bereaved.

The Hares have moved house now, which was both painful and important. It proved helpful in moving them on a stage in their grieving. They have also adopted twin daughters, who were in care and had been ill-treated and badly neglected. In deciding to adopt, Diana was never looking for a replacement for Georgina – that would be impossible – rather she and Tim felt they had something of value to offer – a good home and a lot of love – which was there to be used.

The twins were three when they arrived. Now they are six, and meeting this family for the first time you would not guess the traumas they have all lived through.

It has not been easy. Contrary to what perhaps everyone, including herself, expected, Tim and Charlie found the little girls easier to start with than Diana did. She knew that inevitably there would be difficulties, especially with two little children who had been so traumatized, but said she was unprepared to find herself resenting their use of things that had been Georgina's.

Diana is as honest as she is courageous.

'Sometimes,' she said to me, 'the early days felt interminable. I would feel as though two strange, and very wild, children had been dumped on me for the day – but then there was no one to come and take them away in the evening. Also, with your own baby, you start from a point of love that is already there. This time I had to make that love, and build on it gradually.' The twins are not identical, and an added problem to start with was that one twin had an easier temperament to deal with than the other. A turning point came when this child became very ill and was rushed into hospital. For an awful few hours a kidney infection was queried and Diana felt the whole ghastly hospital crisis syndrome was starting up for her again. Happily it was not so. The child had pneumonia and recovered, but during the time she was ill she suddenly said to Diana, in astonishment, 'Mummy, you really love me enough to stay with me all the time, don't you?' and Diana was able to say, 'Yes, darling. Of course I do' – and know it was true.

Georgina's death has had a profound effect on all the family. Both grandmothers were extremely involved with her during her life and grieved terribly after her death. In adopting the twins it also means that other people in the family circle have had to accept a new relationship too. There have been adjustments, not always easy ones, for everyone to make.

I would regard the Hares as a wonderful example of a family who have put their anguish to a tremendously positive use.

Jane's letter about her son's cot death makes it clear how much the death of her mother, when she was five, has affected her life. Another woman told me how dreadfully isolated she felt, aged twelve, when her father died. It was worst at school because her friends had no idea how to treat her, so she felt that they not only shunned her but also she was a source of fascination to them. I know of one young woman aged nineteen who was deeply affected by the fact that she had not been able to say goodbye to her mother, who died of cancer when the daughter was aged eleven.

One widow told me that her young son, who could cope with her tears at home, had once begged her, 'Please don't cry in the Gondola, Mummy.' I had a vision of her being asked to restrain herself while on a wonderful holiday in Venice, or when swinging about in the confined space of a cable-car in the Alps. It turned out to be a restaurant where they sometimes went for a treat and were liable to meet people they knew. Bereaved parents not only have to cope with their own grief, but that of their children as well. This can be a powerful incentive to get back to normal, the very thing that forces us to keep going, but it can also be a great added burden and responsibility. This story also illustrates that the reverse is true too: children not only have to cope with their own grief, but that of their parents – something difficult and alien to a child. All the same I feel it is important not to shut children out of our grief. As always, it is a difficult balance. We walk a tightrope.

It is tempting to feed children 'certainties' that we do not always feel ourselves. I have no idea if this is right or wrong, but their extremely literal interpretation of our palliative explanations can certainly bring surprises. After my mother's death, I happened to have a small grandson staying with me for a fortnight while I was trying to clear out her flat. As a good Roman Catholic he had received religious instruction. He was much interested in her whereabouts.

'Has Great gone to heaven or hell?' he asked me.

'Heaven,' I said firmly, not feeling capable at that particular moment, as I embarked on the dreary task of sorting out my mother's possessions, of entering into a fascinating discussion about the great mysteries.

'Did the angels take her up on her bed, and then bring the bed back down again?' he asked. I said I didn't know. It was a boiling hot day, and at some stage my sister-in-law, who lived in an adjoining flat, brought us out welcome cold drinks. I thanked her and told her she was an angel.

'What on earth did you tell Freddie about death?' my daughter Susannah asked me later. 'He seems to think Aunt Bud is some sort of removal man who transported Gran up to heaven.'

Two years later this child is still under the impression that he visited heaven at my mother's old flat and saw an angel – nothing we say can shake him on this. Luckily he thought it a blissful experience.

'Do let's have a go on your lovely wheelie climbing frame,' I heard him ask my mother's neighbour, a charming old man with a zimmer, who was obligingly playing a subservient Mrs Noah to my three-year-old grandson's starring role in the drama of the Flood.

'So, are angels the strongest people in the whole world?' another grandchild, always one for following his own train of thought like a bloodhound without reference to anyone else, once asked his mother, apropos of nothing that was being talked about at the time. He saved her from replying by adding, 'They have to be, to get the elephants to heaven.'

Personally, I am quite comfortable with the concept of angelic presences. Perhaps I might not normally visualize them in the guise of removal men – though I don't see why not – but God, if he or she exists, must surely need to delegate. I was amused to hear on my radio this morning that next week is to be designated Angelic Awareness Week! Having written the previous paragraph the night before, I was enchanted by this bit of synchronicity. I shall be on the lookout, though I have a feeling that angels don't appear to order in this way.

Here is a poem I wrote about Amanda.

Why were you born . . .

. . . you who could not stay
with us to share our life
which gave you breath,
and what is death
to those who have not lived?
What did you learn
who did not know man's love
or fear his scorn?
Why were you born?

So short your life
we hardly knew each other,
never shared together
songs or mirth:
only your birth
I shared before a bleak goodbye.
What spark survives
or were those few fraught months,
each day a knife,
your only life?

Where are you now
and can I find you
on the road through life
that I must tread,
or are you dead
that have not sinned
or sacrificed or laughed?
And shall I search for you?
Oh tell me how!

Oh tell me how.

Part Two

For the next few years the period in our lives that had started with the birth of Amanda felt like a roller-coaster of unexpected twists and turns, with sudden ups immediately followed by stomach-churning downs.

The new baby, Susannah, flourished. Belinda was a bewitching bit of quicksilver and we felt wonderfully lucky with our two small girls. While Amanda and all her might-have-beens remained in my thoughts, life seemed rich again, but that period had stirred up a lot of questions. I read avidly about what the different faiths had to say about life after death. I was no longer sure what my own beliefs were. If Amanda had continued in some way, I wondered what was happening to her now.

I am not saying that I lost all faith. Reviewing belief was not a new experience, but it had an added urgency. From my earliest years I had questioned things. My first religious wonderings came when I was six. I had been a bridesmaid, and my mother, instructing me about the marriage service, explained that it enabled children to be born. I clearly remember feeling impressed and thinking God must indeed be true if the promise to live together could cause him to provide babies on the strength of it, so I must have pondered about his existence already. Unlike today, the biological facts of reproduction were not part of most children's education then. A couple of years later, the discovery that the romantic Duke of Monmouth had been born out of wedlock caused me to review the situation. Two of the little girls with whom I did lessons came up with the riveting information that just getting into bed with a man could do the trick, and God had no hand in it at all. As we'd often had their two-year-old brother in bed with us, we were all rather worried about the outcome. I thought my mother must have got the wrong end of the stick about God, and this caused doubts, but not ones I voiced to grown-ups.

The sadness of Amanda did not make me reject the possibility of either God or an afterlife, but at least it made me think. Increasingly I was bothered about prayer, which I had up to now only thought of as a vehicle for requests, a sort of grown-up extension of a list for Father Christmas. I saw no reason why these should be granted, though it didn't stop me trying. I wanted to pray, but no longer felt the old patterns I had grown up with were meaningful. I came to no conclusions, but somehow, somewhere I felt Amanda might still exist and have come for a purpose. It was this longing to know what might have happened to her that caused me anxiety. I found church services difficult, but I think it was the birth and death of Amanda that started me on a spiritual search and made me want to learn about wider views than the rather narrow ones in which I had been brought up. I am grateful for this.

The school was going well. There were plenty of minor dramas and irritations, but there is never a dull moment running a school. The boys were enchanting and funny, and on the whole the parents were delightful; many of them were already friends of Charlie from his Eton, Cambridge or army days, and some others became lifelong friends to us both. Of course, there were those who were less congenial, a few who were tiresome and, very occasionally, one or two whom we actively disliked – but a good hate can be quite enjoyable and no doubt these parents thought we were equally ghastly.

I had started to be uneasy about Charlie well before Susannah was born. He seemed dogged by health problems – pneumonia, pleurisy and intermittent bouts of back trouble, which laid him low and once put him in a plaster cast. I longed for him to be fit, and felt envious of friends who seemed to have a more carefree life. I also felt hurt when he teased that he had never really been ill until he married me. This may not have been without significance. On his own admission he had never before been emotionally involved with a woman, but had coasted along as a light-hearted bachelor. Perhaps the rougher ride of a close personal relationship may have upset his equilibrium. However, there was nothing actually threatening about his malaise, or so I thought.

Then, soon after Susannah arrived, he started having blood in his urine and was very unwell with bouts of cystitis. He went into hospital for tests: a cystoscopy showed nothing sinister. He was given antibiotics and the condition would clear up for a bit and then return.

During that April holidays, my in-laws took me on a Hellenic cruise, and my father, an old friend of theirs, came too. Looking back, it seems a particularly precious holiday: an oasis in a desert.

Neither Charlie nor my mother wanted to come.

My mother, a tremendous home-bird with a strong liking for being in control, always felt threatened off her own patch and said she would prefer to have Nan and the children to stay with her in Wales.

As for Charlie, he liked leading, not following, expeditions. He was in his element climbing off the piste with sealskins under his skis, and then taking a party down an untracked mountainside in powder snow; he liked discovering new places that no one else knew about. He didn't at all take to the idea of being shepherded about by someone else however good the organization might be, but he encouraged me to accept the invitation.

He visited his sister in Ireland while the children were with my mother, and then spent the rest of the holidays with them at the school, dotingly cared for by Nan, immersing himself happily in his beloved garden – as far as I know the only real rival I ever had for his love – while I enjoyed myself in Greece.

The average age on the SS *Ankara* was high and I was probably the youngest passenger on board. My aunt-in-law, at eighty, was the life and soul of the party, never flagging no matter how early the start or arduous the expedition. I felt as though I had temporarily packed up my troubles and anxieties, and it was the greatest fun.

My elderly companions spoilt me rotten, the sites we visited were fascinating, the weather fabulous, the lectures excellent and we were wonderfully well looked after – indeed, we were so nannied and taken care of that my father said he expected someone to ask him if he'd 'been' after breakfast and to tick his name off on a list!

As my father and uncle-in-law were classical scholars, it was like having my own personal guides as well as the official tour ones.

My father wandered round in a happy trance, quoting

Homer at the drop of a hat and trying to converse in ancient Greek with surprised and uncomprehending locals, though he was pleased when he managed to translate the description on an advertisement for instant coffee as 'ground unto dust'. One evening, when a thunderstorm threatened and a purple cloud hung overhead, he was enchanted to verify the colour of Homer's 'wine-dark' sea. He was somewhat disappointed, however, to find that the small, dark, hirsute Mediterranean people who scurried round twentieth-century Athens bore little resemblance to the golden athletes of his imagination. I think he had always envisaged his Olympian heroes as a race of tall, fair Rupert Brooke types, only more beefy – a sort of super first XI of perfect English schoolboys. He wept unashamedly when the *Nostos* of Odysseus was read aloud to us, but as very few of the other assembled passengers could understand a word of it, they looked at this display of emotion in some surprise.

They were even more surprised during a lull in conversation at dinner one night, when it was announced that we were sailing past the island of Lesbos, and my aunt-in-law, looking round at the large number of middle-aged ladies on board, announced in a ringing voice, 'And I should think a good many of the passengers ought to be put off here!' Discussion of homosexual relationships was not a common part of conversation at that time.

One morning my father, wearing his old Jaeger dressing-gown and with his sparse supply of hair standing on end, appeared in my cabin at dawn and said, 'A white dove has just landed on my head.' I thought the whole experience of visiting so many places about which he had taught for so many years, but never before seen, must have flipped his trip switch completely. I made soothing noises.

'No, no,' he said crossly. 'Don't be so silly. It really happened. Come up on deck and look.' I followed him out, and there, sure enough, was an exhausted white pigeon. It must have been blown off course, sighted the ship with relief, and homed in to the spot where my father's bald head gleamed in the early morning light.

I picked the bird up and hoped it was a lucky omen.

At the end of the cruise, my father and Uncle Charles flew home and Aunt Evelyn and I stayed on for a few days in Venice. I hope she got as much pleasure from showing me this city of dreams as I got from my first visit, though I suddenly longed desperately for Charlie to be with me. I had not pined for him while we were on the cruise. I think we had needed that short space from each other, but Venice is a romantic city and I missed my mate. I was longing to be with him and the children again.

As far as I remember, the summer term passed without any particular drama, though I do know that I felt Charlie was not back to his true self. I couldn't put my finger on what was wrong, but he seemed distant in some way and I felt unsatisfied and anxious.

We were racing at Goodwood at the beginning of the summer holidays when the real trouble started. Charlie was the racing enthusiast, and though I enjoyed the jaunt, I was never hooked, so I was surprised when he suggested we should go home halfway through the day.

When we got home he said to me, 'Something is very wrong. I can't pee.' He looked awful and was in great pain. Duncan McNeill arrived and was on the telephone within minutes of seeing Charlie, trying to find a hospital bed.

There was none available locally, and it was to a hospital considerably further afield that he was rushed. I had no idea where the hospital was and, as I followed the ambulance in my car, I was terrified I would lose it as it shot through red lights, bells ringing. This was the first of several such occasions in my life. It is not a pastime I recommend.

The surgeon expected to find, and remove, a prematurely enlarged prostate gland. He explained to me that Charlie could still be potent, but it would mean we could have no more children together. My reaction to this was violent. We had intended to try for another baby sometime. I had been in no hurry, but now I became obsessed with a desperate longing for a baby.

I had the weirdest thoughts and felt like a tigress robbed of her cubs, as though I was being cheated of my birthright. I am neither excusing nor defending this feeling of mine, I who was lucky enough to have two children already. I am simply stating what I felt. What it did show me, for the few days when Charlie was in hospital before the operation, was an inkling of how deeply primitive and physical – an all-consuming hunger – the longing for a child must be for those who try to achieve one and cannot do so.

In fact, Charlie's condition, although it would not affect his ability to father a child as a prostate operation would have done, was much more serious. He had malignant papillomas in his bladder, which should have shown up earlier through the cystoscope. When I enquired why they had not done so, the surgeon admitted that they were awkwardly and unusually placed, and had he used an instrument which gave a completely all-round view the first time, he would have been able to spot them. I thought it was very honest of him to admit this to me.

Charlie had to have more than half his bladder removed. It was a terrible shock to be told he had cancer. In 1960 it was not the open subject it is today. It was spoken of, if at all, in hushed whispers, but all the same it came as a surprise to me that the doctor did not intend to tell Charlie the true diagnosis. He said the prognosis was poor and the degree of malignancy was serious. This reticence would be highly unusual now, and though I think today's greater openness is right, I wonder if the pendulum has swung too far, as pendulums have a nasty way of doing. There is a difference between a realistic assessment and taking hope away. Some doctors are understandably afraid of raising false optimism, but raising despair seems even more dangerous to me. Hope is a very powerful weapon.

I was terribly frightened. I sat by Charlie, willing him to live. This was my first taste of the helpless feeling of keeping watch by my best-beloved when he was really ill, longing to help and support, but receiving little apparent response to indicate if I was being of comfort. I am not talking about children here: mothers instinctively know that their presence is a valuable, even vital, aid to recovery. It can undoubtedly be true with adults too, but I longed for some feedback, a reassurance that I was contributing to Charlie's recovery. I was to learn that when people are fighting for their lives, they do not have much energy to show response.

Nowadays techniques and post-operative care have greatly improved and patients are sent home much sooner after major operations but, then, Charlie was in hospital for several weeks. I have some very unhappy memories of sitting by his bed feeling panic-stricken, useless and very lonely, but trying not to show it. I so badly wanted to be hopeful, but sometimes I couldn't help my imagination racing along to deathbed scenes, and though I hated myself for this, there was an awful, compelling fascination about it.

One evening, on my way home after leaving the hospital, I drove the wrong way round a roundabout. Luckily there was nothing coming.

There were some brighter moments, though. The senior nurse was a man – unusual then – with the splendid name of Charge-Nurse Rutter, though most patients incongruously addressed him as Sister. He led an improbable double life: part of the time he ran the men's surgical ward with super efficiency, and the rest of the time he was a professional comic appearing in variety shows at a pier on the south coast. Apparently the two timetables dovetailed perfectly. He used to try his latest wisecracks out on Charlie and me; no doubt he picked up a good deal of copy for his scripts from his patients and their families. He was an extremely funny man and a wonderful nurse. He cheered us up no end.

Perhaps a course in comic patter should be a compulsory part of a nurse's training. There is, after all, the well-documented case of the American journalist Norman Cousins, who, faced with a life-threatening disease and the doctors' admission that they could do no more for him, took himself out of hospital, hired masses of videos that amused him and literally laughed himself better. Laughter, like hope, is a powerful drug too.

There was a gruesome old man called Fred at the hospital, the possessor of ominously shaky hands, who came to shave the male patients with a cut-throat razor. He made grizzly jokes about slitting throats, and I felt he might have been descended from the gravediggers in *Hamlet*. I held my breath as I watched him wobbling towards my precious husband, razor in hand, and begged Charlie to grow a beard;

Charlie, always a sucker for adventure, couldn't quite resist the excitement.

I decided that if Charlie himself was not to know he had cancer, then I would tell as few people as possible, and no one at or connected with the school. I made up my mind that if Charlie ever asked a direct question I would tell him the truth, but meanwhile, if I had to act a lie, I would make that lie as convincing as I could – a brilliant lie – and try to surround him with optimism. I felt that if he saw me exuding happy confidence, it would be infectious. He never asked either me or any of the doctors or nurses any questions at all.

It was not till a consultant was reviewing his medical history after his first big coronary, years later, that we discussed it together. I asked Charlie then if he'd secretly always suspected the truth and he said yes, but that as he didn't want to know, he'd simply decided not to think about it. This was typical of him, a deliberate ostrich act that was a brilliant coping strategy for him – albeit sometimes maddening – but one that I did not possess. I tended to rush round flinging open every possible cupboard door in a manic search for suspected skeletons. I have grown a little more circumspect with age.

All those years later, Charlie was astonished to learn that I'd always known about the cancer. He didn't think I would have been capable of keeping the information to myself – not very flattering!

After our carefree Hellenic cruise, my aunt-in-law had come back to have a sudden cancer operation herself, so I felt the least I could do for the time being was to spare my in-laws additional anxiety. They knew about Charlie's operation, but not how serious his condition was. As papillomas can be non-malignant this was not a difficult deception.

A school, empty of its usual occupants, can be an echoing, lifeless place, but I took refuge with the children when I was not at the hospital. As always, Nan was a tower of strength. Though I was relieved not to have to cope with the term-time demands of running a large establishment, without my usual busy routine there was a lot of time to worry about the future. Normally we never stayed at the school during the holidays except for a few days at the beginning and end, but divided our time between Charlie's family in Yorkshire and mine in Wales.

When Charlie came home I tried to be bright and cheerful, but all his energies were still going into his fight to get better and there seemed little spark left for me. Longing for comfort myself, I resented this. Although I think I put on a reasonable outward show, I hated the hidden self-pity that clung round me like a fog, and my vision of myself as a brave little ray of sunshine took a fearful battering.

Eventually Charlie was well enough to travel. We took the children to my parents in Wales, and life improved. Charlie had been told that he would have to go into hospital for a cystoscopy inspection under general anaesthetic first every three, then later, every six months. If he remained clear for five years – very good news – then this would be cut down to once a year. This would not be necessary now because blood and urine tests have become so much more sophisticated and accurate. The first test at three months was clear. I began to hope.

The next drama to hit us was that Susannah became extremely ill with a severe attack of the diarrhoea and vomiting epidemic that was going round at the time. The doctor had seen her and given her an injection, but I shall never forget the horrifying speed with which she suddenly seemed to shrink before my eyes as I tramped the floor with her one night. It was as though a rosy summer apple turned in seconds into a wizened winter one that had been stored too long. Another dash to hospital followed and we thought we were going to lose this child too.

The doctors were unable to get the life-saving drip in her leg for a terrifying two hours – a problem with difficult veins which has caused her trouble since and which she shared with Charlie. The medical team fought for her life for the next forty-eight hours. At one moment they insisted that I should go home for a few hours' rest and with one accord Charlie and I drove to the nearest church to pray for her. Despite my doubts it was our automatic reaction to do this.

I do not for a moment think prayers could be more effective because they are prayed inside a church. It was sheer desperation that sent us there, but I would have been devastated if we'd been unable to get in. This experience has left me with a bee that still buzzes round my bonnet: I feel strongly that church doors should be open. Lock the valuables up by all means, but not the doors, otherwise surely the whole point of the building is denied. This is not a view I have found popular with most parochial church councils.

Soon after Susannah recovered, another disaster struck. During these difficult times I was lucky to have two exceptional women working for me: one was my children's nanny, Nan, and the other was Val, the wife of the school handyman. Val had scooped me up and seen me through my first year of married life, when I found it extremely difficult living not so much over the shop as actually in it.

In the 1950s, when headmasters or clergymen married, it was automatically assumed that their wives would take on the job as well as the man, though I suppose most headmasters' wives had a more gradual progress to the position than I did. At twenty-one I was very bolshie about the lack of privacy in our living quarters, and about other people's expectations of what my role should be.

I seemed to spend the first year of marriage in either fits of laughter, because I thought all the ruffled feathers and petty feuds in a small residential community were so hilarious, or floods of tears because I thought it was all so awful – there was not much calm water in between these two extremes. Poor Charlie! It must have been a shock to have imported this sharp-angled peg into such a rigidly round hole. If Charlie and I had not always had the power to make each other laugh and enjoyed each other's company so much, it might have ended in disaster. It nearly did.

Luckily, as the years went by, the round hole got more pliable, and the peg had a few of her corners knocked off, but to begin with it was Val's astringent support and love that helped me cope.

She had a wonderfully zany sense of humour and a sardonic view of most other members of staff. She was also fiercely loyal to me, and no doubt completely biased about what she perceived my interests to be. She had two little girls, the younger one a year older than Belinda, and this was another link between us.

Val, like Nan, had been a huge support over Amanda, and more recently had helped me nurse Charlie with great devotion. Now she suddenly became ill herself, and disclosed that for some time she'd had several large lumps in various parts of her body about which she had said nothing. Unbeknownst to the rest of us she had previously had a large wart-type growth removed from her arm and had been told to return for check-ups but had not done so. The word cancer had never been mentioned to her, though her medical records now revealed that it had been a malignant melanoma. Her poor husband, Bill, the weaker one of the partnership, whom she had always carried, and for whose shortcomings she had often covered up, went to pieces.

Val died two months later in the Hammersmith Hospital. We kept her at home as long as we could, but if ever anyone needed the loving skill of a hospice such as would have been available now, she did. The last time I saw her, the day before she died, I sat and held the hand of an almost unrecognizable skeleton in an enormous and busy ward. 'No one will ever know how bad I feel. No one,' were her last whispered words to me. They have haunted me ever since.

I missed her terribly. We tried to help her family, but Bill, who had always been unreliable (he could be good on his day, but you never knew when he was going to have one), now found coping with job and family too much, and left to live nearer to relations. He turned out not to have been married to Val after all, and was supposed to be paying maintenance to another family. I realized that while giving me so much devotion and support, Val had been carrying terrible anxieties and burdens of her own about which she never breathed a word. I came to guess things had been far worse in many ways than I knew, and longed to have her back and have the chance to do more for her, and redress the balance somewhat.

I thought nothing else could go wrong after this, but we were not to be allowed a lull.

Soon after the Christmas holidays, Charlie had another stoppage, was rushed to hospital again and a return of the cancer was diagnosed. The surgeon who had operated before recommended complete removal of the bladder, which seemed a gloomy option. He was extremely understanding and generous when Duncan McNeill and I decided to ask for another opinion, and made it easy for us to do so. I felt very grateful for this. Charlie came home to spend several weeks in bed, attached to a catheter, while we waited for a place in the Middlesex Hospital in London, where he was to be seen by Sir Eric Ritches.

Sir Eric became our hero. Though full of praise for the surgical skill with which the previous operation had been carried out, Eric disagreed with the surgeon's verdict. To our great relief, he decided to do another partial cystectomy and not to remove the whole bladder, with all the misery and inconvenience that this would have meant for the rest of Charlie's life. If part of an organ has to be removed, the bladder is not a bad one to choose: being inflatable it eventually stretches again, though it is agonizingly uncomfortable and presents many problems during the interim period.

Friends gave me a permanent bed in their London house so that I could come and go freely, and divide my time between Charlie and the children without making complicated plans. I shall never forget their kindness.

Charlie started the tedious slog to recovery again. I longed desperately to be free of hospitals: their very particular smell makes my stomach churn to this day. I longed to be carefree. I felt out of step with many of my friends whose lives seemed more light-hearted, but I did not want to turn into a dreary moaner, so I tried hard to be outwardly cheerful. Charlie never complained and was completely stoical but I sometimes felt shut out and wanted him to discuss his feelings with me. Acting a lie is lonely.

It might be worth recording that during this time my brother, David, to whom I have always been very close, had a vivid experience. He was sitting at his desk about to write and commiserate with me, when he suddenly became over-whelmed by a feeling of absolute certainty that Charlie's cancer would never recur. Not a hopeful hunch, but a total certainty: a 'knowing', which he could not account for. Any-one who knows David, a man of action if ever there was one, would agree that he is not exactly given to whimsy, but he described it afterwards as being the sort of experience most clergymen would give their eye-teeth to have. He rang me up. Although I couldn't share his certainty, I found it deeply comforting. He was to be proved right.

One morning, about a week after Charlie's second big operation, I received a letter from Aunt Evelyn in Yorkshire. Her cancer had returned and gone to her liver. She had been told she probably had a week to live. Could I possibly come up to Arthington? It was a touching letter saying how much my marriage to Charlie had meant to her. She wanted to say a personal goodbye. Of course I went.

Although she was eighty-one, I could not believe that the acerbic and witty companion of the Hellenic cruise was about to depart so soon. She had seemed indestructible. I hated leaving Charlie, but he very much wanted me to go, not only to see her, but to support his uncle, whom we both loved dearly and knew would be very lost and anxious.

I was worried as to how to behave on being summoned

to a deathbed. I need not have been afraid, and I have always been grateful for the privilege of being with someone who feared death so little, was so matter-of-fact about it and talked about the prospect so openly. She was hugely pleased to see me and said, 'Lovely you managed to make it in time, darling', as though I might have been late for a party.

During the next few days she spoke about her readiness to go, her confident hope that she would be reunited in some way with those she had loved in her life. 'I feel as if I have come down a long dark tunnel lately,' she said. 'And there is now a bright light at the end. Sometimes I can see it. The only thing that would frighten me is to have to crawl back up and make this dark journey again.'

I had always been terrified of dying. As a small child I remember deliberately fighting sleep for fear that once I lost consciousness I might never regain it. I think this set the pattern for the sleep problems that have plagued me all my life. I gather it is unusual to fear death quite so dramatically at so early an age. I certainly never told my always sympathetic mother or anyone else about it. I can think of several possible explanations. One is that I often experienced a terrifying sensation, just before I fell asleep, when I felt as if I was going to burst out of my body. I could feel myself swelling, my hands in particular, and felt myself rushing away while everything in the room round me grew smaller and more distant. Then I would 'come back' and would scream and scream. The grown-ups always thought I had nightmares, but I knew with certainty that it happened when I was awake. Now I think I may have been on the verge of having out-of-the-body experiences but never quite made it! I grew out of this secret misery and almost forgot about it, until I became extremely ill with infective hepatitis, soon after Charlie and I were married, and it returned. If I am very over-tired, I still, occasionally, feel this horrible and frightening sensation coming on, but I can consciously control it now. There are other possible explanations I can think of, but I suspect this might be the chief one. Perhaps I was just a highly strung and over-imaginative child.

Anyway, those few days spent with Aunt Evelyn did a lot to take the fear of death away – not the fear of the process of dying, but of actual death itself.

I knew it was a comfort to Uncle Charles to have me there, which compensated somewhat for my anguish in having to abandon Charlie. No in-laws could ever have made anyone feel more loved than this bachelor and spinster pair had always made me feel.

Oddly enough, despite the potential sadness of my errand, we had quite a hilarious few days, but when I left Arthington I felt very harrowed and hated saying goodbye. I knew I would probably not see Aunt Evelyn again. I said to Uncle Charles, 'Ring me night or day if you need me and I will try to come back.'

I returned to London and the Middlesex Hospital. Sir Eric Ritches was pleased with his patient. He told me he thought Charlie had amazing recuperative powers. Many other doctors were to say the same thing over the years. I remember feeling put out that Charlie did not seem to understand what life looked like through my eyes at the time, and appeared to me to be more concerned with what was going on in the hospital than with the juggling act I felt I was performing between him, our children, his family and what I crossly called 'his' school. The nurses all adored him: he was their star patient.

It occurred to me that however sad the situation in

Yorkshire was, however unhappy I felt, on another level I had not been averse to the fuss that was made of me. Everyone likes to be told they're wonderful. I had been the star in Yorkshire: Charlie was the star here. I realized I was jealous.

I went home to spend Easter with the children in an extremely humbled and sober frame of mind.

Early on Easter Monday I was awakened by the telephone. I grabbed it, heart hammering, instantly wide awake. My first thought, that it might be about Charlie, was immediately followed by the expectation that it must be news of Aunt Evelyn's death.

It was neither. Uncle Charles had been discovered slumped over the telephone in the hall by Cissie Jackson, their devoted parlour-maid who had worked for them for fifty years. She thought he must have been trying to ring the doctor, but I knew with absolute certainty that he would have been trying to ring me. I wished he had been able to get through to me. He was still breathing but barely conscious. Cissie Jackson's old voice cracked on the telephone – would I come back at once?

Being a bank holiday, all the flights to Leeds were booked, but I got the earliest train I could and was in Leeds by the afternoon. I was just too late. Uncle Charles had died an hour before I got there. I minded more than I can say that I had not been able to bring him some last-minute comfort.

I felt as if my world was disintegrating. I went upstairs to Aunt Evelyn, dreading how I would find her.

'Hello, darling. Uncle has rather stolen my thunder, hasn't he?' she said.

*

Many people had been wonderfully supportive to me, but the kindness of one childhood friend of Charlie's, Michael, an eminent surgeon in Leeds whose son was a pupil at the school, has to have special mention. He had constantly rung up to know how Charlie was progressing, and it had been comforting for me, with my self-imposed rule not to disclose the truth about the diagnosis, to be able to discuss my queries and anxieties over Charlie's cancer with an expert. He had also promised to keep in touch with my in-laws, of whom he was very fond. He not only met my train at Leeds that Easter Monday, but came back to Arthington with me and announced that until my sister-in-law could get over from Ireland to help me, he was going to come and sleep in the house each night because he thought I was under too much strain. I protested that I could cope perfectly well, but he insisted. He came each evening after dinner for the next few nights. I hardly saw him. He was gone before seven in the morning, but the relief of knowing that there was someone there to share the responsibility with me was enormous. I still think this was an amazingly imaginative gesture from an exceedingly busy man. It was also very generous of his wife and family to let him make it.

There was one thing, however, that he protected me from which I think it would have been better if he'd helped me to face, though he acted out of the purest kindness and concern for me.

I had never seen a dead body and was secretly terrified at the prospect. Aunt Evelyn asked me to go and see if Uncle Charles looked peaceful. She also asked me to make sure that his doctor came to slit a vein to be certain he was 'really dead' – a request that made my hair stand on end. I asked Michael if he would come in to Uncle Charles's bedroom with me, but he was emphatic that I should not go in, an insistence which actually fuelled my dread. He said he would see that all was well and reassure Aunt Evelyn, but knowing as I do now that there is nothing to be afraid of in seeing a body, provided that there is no disfigurement, I wish I had insisted on going with him. Imagination – mine anyway – usually conjures up bogeys that are much worse than reality, and it would have put a stop to a deep fear of mine. I also felt I failed my aunt-in-law at the very end of her life by avoiding this request of hers. I have always regretted that.

I had no idea how hectic the first week after a death can be, or how complicated it is to arrange a funeral and try to please a number of different interested parties, not all of whom are on the spot.

Aunt Evelyn, dying upstairs but absolutely in control mentally, had strong ideas herself – she always had strong ideas about everything. It was one of the things that made her such fun, though a number of people were absolutely terrified of her sharp tongue. I was lucky. By the time I appeared on the scene she had given up hope of Charlie making it to the altar, and was so enchanted by the idea of him acquiring a wife that she was predisposed in my favour from the start, and was never anything but a boon companion to me.

She had introduced me to all sorts of new interests, including psychical research and the paranormal, and became for me that most special person – a book-swapping chum. She adored anything new, from the latest novel to a new play, a car to a toaster. She had a television of giant proportions long before most people had a set at all, loved going to exhibitions and was mad about the cinema. When-ever I came to stay we used to jaunt off to the latest film together in her spanking new Morris Minor car, weaving thrillingly across the tramlines that still existed in Leeds, and progressing in a series of alarming kangaroo jumps because she adored the surge of power that a violent short pressure on the accelerator gave her. She had been one of the first women students at Lady Margaret Hall, had played hockey for Yorkshire, ridden to hounds, been a compulsive gambler on the horses at one stage, travelled widely and she was an avid reader.

Despite all this activity I think she was probably happier in old age than at any time in her life. As an unmarried daughter living at home, she'd had independent means financially but no real independence till late middle age, when her mother died: at forty she was still expected to report back to this minuscule but formidable lady if she had even been out to dinner. She had a first-class brain, an inquiring mind, and though she did quite a lot of charity work, she had no real committed outlet for her energy. Nowadays she would unquestionably have had a career, probably of some distinction. She was cruelly considered 'plain' in her youth, and had been, I suspect, very frustrated sexually. Apparently she had been desperately jealous of my beautiful, widowed mother-in-law for whom men fell like ninepins, and Charlie, who adored his mother, had never quite forgiven his aunt for the difficulties she caused her.

During her last week of life, Aunt Evelyn told me how much she regretted many small but sharp unkindnesses and thanked me for being a bridge between Charlie and herself in the last few years. I deserved no credit. It was easy for me, who had never been on the receiving end of her poisoned-arrow words, and to whom she was never anything but delightful. I owe her a debt of gratitude as someone who opened new windows in my mind.

It was a great relief when my sister-in-law, Rosemary, arrived for Uncle Charles's funeral, and I felt the burden of responsibility was lifted.

Despite my experience, through Amanda, of the strange fluctuations of grief, I was surprised to find how numb I felt about the death of my much-loved uncle-in-law.

Though he shared a marvellous sense of humour with her, he could hardly have been a more different character from his sister. Understatement was his hallmark and he had none of her flamboyance or streak of bullying. He was one of the kindest men I knew, but behind a deadpan expression, he was also a great tease. When I first met him I was enormously gullible, not to say naïve, but it didn't take me long to discover that I was swallowing dollops of moonshine, to his huge amusement. I got his measure, and we became devoted to each other. Despite his unassuming manner he could be a force to be reckoned with, and the Colonel, as he was known locally, was held in great respect. Charlie wrote to Aunt Evelyn from his hospital bed, 'Uncle Charles has always been my guiding star and my yardstick in all matters of integrity.' He was specially loved by those lucky enough to get to know him well – a darling man.

The church was packed for his funeral. Uncle Charles, the humblest of men, would have been astounded. I was completely thrown by the service and my floodgates opened. I was mortified that the first tears I had shed for him should be such public ones, but once started I couldn't stop.

At the funeral, Dennis Wilkinson, a great family friend, and, like my father and Uncle Charles, a retired Eton housemaster, collapsed and died of a heart attack during the service. It must have been ghastly for Gillian, his wife.

I felt we had a jinx on us and wondered if I was a

catalyst for trouble. At some time during this period I ran over a dog which rushed out suddenly from the hedge and literally went under the wheels of my car. I remember thinking, 'Poor animal. It crossed my path. What else could it expect?' Melodramatic perhaps, but it did seem as if the old Grim Reaper had gone wild with a combine harvester and was busy roaring around in it wherever I happened to be.

The day after the funeral was a Sunday, and Rosemary and I went to church, and sat together in the pew at the front which the family had always occupied. We wore black, as was still common in the fifties, and were feeling very sad, but when a high-pitched note on the organ stuck at the start of the sermon, drowning the vicar's frantic efforts to compete with it, we both got the most terrible attack of church giggles, and I remember crying, not this time with grief, but with suppressed laughter. We got some disapproving looks, except from the ancient organist, George Proctor, a particular pal of mine, who turned round and gave me a huge wink. He'd probably pulled the note out on purpose, though whether to cheer me up or because he couldn't stand the vicar, I wasn't sure. They fought a running battle and George sometimes deliberately played the wrong chant for the psalm just for the hell of it, and frequently started the last hymn before the sermon was over.

I went back to London to collect Charlie from the hospital at long last, and to take him home. I should have felt excited but I just felt punch-drunk. My sister-in-law stayed on at Arthington.

A few days later Aunt Evelyn died, and this time I drove Charlie up to Yorkshire with me. There was a terrible sense of *déjà vu* as we went through another funeral. It also marked the end of an era.

On the death of his aunt and uncle, Charlie inherited the Sheepshanks family home, the Arthington Estate. It had been bought early in the nineteenth century by Charlie's great-great-grandfather. Charlie's own father had died when his eldest son was aged four, Charlie aged two, and my sister-in-law, Rosemary, was only a fortnight old.

My poor mother-in-law, Olive Sheepshanks, certainly had her share of tragedy. Her firstborn, Dick, a legend in his own short lifetime as an athlete, a wit, a 'deb's delight' and a brilliant young war correspondent with Reuters, was to be killed aged twenty-seven in the Spanish Civil War. It was thought at the time that a stray shell landed on the car in which he and three other journalists were travelling, though an allegation has since been made that he might have been murdered by Kim Philby – the only one of the four young men to survive this disaster – but that is another story. Olive brought up her family in a house on the estate, very much in the shadow of a powerful mother-in-law and a jealous sister-in-law, with no husband to support her.

By the time I knew her, my mother-in-law was suffering from what I'm now sure was Alzheimer's disease. At our wedding she had asked a surprised guest who the bride and groom were, and after we were married used to complain to Charlie that she kept finding 'this girl' (me) in his bedroom, and would he please get rid of her!

I wish I'd been older, wiser and more tolerant; it is one of my regrets that I did not deal better with this situation. It must have been impossible for Charlie, loving us both so much, but caught between the two of us – the one deranged and bewildered, the other baffled and hurt. I'm afraid I had some severe sense of humour failures over her behaviour. When we were engaged, I had once gone, unwillingly, to have lunch *à deux* with her, and was extremely disconcerted when she opened a tin of dog meat for us both: no book of etiquette that I'd read had armed me for that eventuality.

She died a year after we married, and I felt nothing but relief. Had I known her before her mind started to disintegrate and her character to change, I'm sure I would have loved her. Those who did said she was enchanting. Even in the sad, muddled, and frequently difficult, phase of her last years, a flicker of her old charm would occasionally appear to flash across the scene with the brilliance of a dragonfly's flight. Alzheimer's is a cruel disease.

There were many decisions to be taken about Arthington. My in-laws had moved out of the big house soon after war began, and like so many other owners of large country houses, had lent it as a military hospital for the duration. After the war was over, they couldn't face the upheaval of moving back into it, and had let it on a twenty-year lease to the West Riding County Council as a men's convalescent hospital. We had all assumed they would want to renew this lease, but only a few months before Uncle Charles's death, he heard that it was no longer required. Efforts to let it to some other institution had proved fruitless, and he had been very bothered about what to do with it.

It was now in bad repair, smothered in dark green and margarine paint, which the hospital had used during the war, and to eyes not wearing rose-tinted spectacles, I suppose it looked pretty grim. My spectacles were fluorescent pink.

We wondered if we could divide it up, live in one part

ourselves and let the rest of it as flats. Friends of ours had successfully done the same sort of thing. Well-meaning close friends and relations, the few who were in the know about Charlie, unwisely took it upon themselves to warn me privately of the folly of even contemplating living in such a huge white elephant of a house. The argument was always the same. 'Face the fact that you are likely to be left a widow with two small children. For heaven's sake don't do anything silly.'

I knew how much Charlie loved the place and, besides, I have always had a weakness for white elephants. Doing something silly became a crusade with me, my own personal gesture of defiance against Charlie's cancer: two fingers up at a fate I was determined should not happen to him. It is hard to explain how important this seemed to me. In theory I knew my kind advisers were sensible and right, but I had a deeply felt hunch that if I could only be brave enough – foolhardy might be a better word – to take a blind leap of faith, then it might, just might, be rewarded.

I find taking decisions extremely hard, and I am not normally at all an implacable character. Indeed, my family tease me about being an incurable mediator, a peacemaker who irritatingly sees the other point of view, so when the blurb on my first novel described it as being about 'the art of compromise', they all fell about with laughter and said, 'Typical Mum!' However, if I do get an inner compulsion, I have also discovered that I disregard it at my peril. I have a theory – not one Charlie appreciated, as it could prove expensive – that it is not giving in to your impulses that you regret: they show what you really want. It is taking the second-best option that bugs one afterwards. This may not seem to tally with my belief in compromise, and I realize that

I am splitting such a fine hair that no one except me may be able to see the two different strands.

We discussed the possibilities for Arthington endlessly.

It took a long time for Charlie to recover from this second big operation. Funerals and bereavements are not ideal therapy for convalescents.

The doctors insisted that we took a proper holiday even though it meant missing the first few weeks of the summer term. Generous parents of a boy in the school lent us their chalet in Gstaad. We both adored the Alps, though, of course, there was no possibility of skiing this time. I had never been to Switzerland in early May before, and it was utterly beautiful. However, though it had its good moments, I do not look back on that luxurious holiday as a happy time.

Charlie was still physically frail, and I suppose I was drained and depressed myself. I know that what I really longed to do was to go wild and let my hair down – to be frivolous, go out dancing, and generally behave in a young and irresponsible way. I couldn't help feeling angry that this was not possible, though goodness knows it was through no fault of Charlie.

We started off on the wrong foot as soon as we arrived. There were two master double bedrooms and both had been got ready. The caretaker asked us if we wanted to use both, or if we only required one. It was Charlie who said we wanted both. We had been told by the doctors that there could be no question of sex for at least three months, and anyway, owing to his illness this had been a no-go area for some time, so that was not the issue. Had he said that if we shared a bed, he might find this restriction difficult, I would have understood and accepted it, but he didn't put it like that. He said it would be more restful to be separate. The fact that this was probably true and that he desperately needed peace did nothing to help me. After weeks of separation and loneliness, I was mortally hurt – but too proud to let him see. I said brightly that I absolutely agreed – so how could I expect him to guess how I felt? But I did. We kissed goodnight, shut our separate doors, and I cried and cried.

Sitting in the sun on the balcony each morning, looking out at snow-capped peaks against a gentian-blue sky, while we ate hot croissants and did *The Times* crossword together ought to have been wonderful.

I would give a great deal to be able to do just that with Charlie now.

Even then I was deeply ashamed that it didn't seem enough, when I knew I was lucky to have him with me at all. I felt terribly churned up inside: to have willed him to live with great passion, only to find myself full of grudges towards him, was an extremely disconcerting experience. The fact that I could not talk freely to him about my anxieties over his cancer did not help, and from that point of view the secrecy made life more difficult for me, but from the point of view of his recovery, I'm still sure it was the right decision for him.

I hated myself and resented what Charlie's illness had done to us both, but outwardly I tried – by no means always successfully – to keep up a bright pretence that all was well. Inwardly I felt a real old misery-guts. I counted my many blessings – and they gazed reproachfully back at my lack of gratitude.

I can see now that I was suffering from a huge reaction after a long period of stress, but stress was not a word we bandied about at that time.

*

We returned to the school and things began to get back to normal. If it was not the best holiday of our lives, the break had, in fact, done us both good. Nan took a long and well-deserved holiday, and it was heaven to be with Belinda and Susannah again.

Nan, as she liked to be called, or Marian Stewart to give her real but seldom used name, had come to us when Belinda was born. She had a face from a Rembrandt painting from which the light shone: she probably taught me more about loving – real, unconditional, unpossessive loving – than anyone else in my life. She was a saint: bearded, deaf-aided and six foot two, with huge ungainly feet. She wore vast tailored suits and a squashy, navy-blue felt hat when she went out, and striped dresses covered with a white apron, indoors. Her shoes, a special laced-up surgical kind, with a built-up heel on one foot, were of a variety designed by a long-dead orthopaedic specialist called Sir Herbert Barker, and were known reverently as 'my Sir Herbert's'. Her hair was scraped back in a bun and she had the most wonderful blue eyes I have ever seen. My little girls thought she was beautiful and they were right. We all adored her.

When I first interviewed Marian Stewart, I hadn't the faintest idea what questions I ought to ask her, so I enquired if she could make toffee on wet afternoons. She said she could. I told her, hesitantly, how much I wanted to be involved with my baby, to look after it as much as possible myself, but that I had a time-consuming job in the school and needed help. I had seen only one other applicant, who had chilled me to the marrow by announcing graciously that she did not object if 'the mummies' occasionally dropped in to nursery tea. But, 'We'll love your babies together,' said Nan, and that is exactly what we did.

Despite her Scottish-sounding name, Nan was a Cornishwoman who had started out as a nursery-maid at fourteen. Her chief duty had been washing linoleum floors with milk. Judging by the awful sour smell which never disappeared when one of my daughters once spilt a pint of milk in a car, I can't help wondering if those grand nurseries were rather pongy. She had graduated to head nurse and worked for years for the Bolitho family in Cornwall. What we all learnt about a character called Morwenna Bolitho, from the working of her bowels to her prowess at cartwheels, would fill several tomes.

By the time Nan came to us, her sister Hilda was cook to a wealthy elderly couple who lived in great state in Hill Street, Mayfair. Nan used to stagger back from days off spent with Hilda, loaded with chocolate cake and shortbread. 'Her Ladyship' apparently wouldn't countenance (countenance was a great word of Nan's) the reappearance of any cake that had even the smallest slice out of it, and the staff felt insulted if any reject from the drawing-room was served up in the 'Servant's Hall' more than once. It was all very *Upstairs, Downstairs*, but we didn't suffer from their inhibitions and happily gobbled up the leftovers.

Nan was a Mrs Malaprop with an endearing tendency to use, or pronounce, words slightly wrong, and had an eccentric way with the placing of aitches. She was hooked on the weather forecast. 'Gorgeous day, Nan,' I would say, angling for the response, 'Ah, but East Angela has floods, Mummy' or 'London Hairport is closed with fog.' Aged two, Belinda christened one of her teddy bears London Hairport. Another one, a particularly noxious pink creature, she named Ambrosia, which gave my father false hopes that we might have a potential classical scholar in the family. He was disappointed to discover this particular bear derived its name from a tin of creamed rice pudding.

Nan had been engaged to her childhood sweetheart for three years when war broke out, but her selfish and authoritarian father refused to let them marry. Her fiancé was taken prisoner by the Japanese and died on the Burma road. From the photograph she always carried with her, he looked very handsome, but I always thought that he must also have been a truly discriminating chap: Nan wasn't exactly a sex kitten to look at, and many men might not have considered her – but she would have been a pearl without price as a wife.

'If we'd only been married for the three months before he went overseas, we could at least have had that time together – and I might have had a little one of my very own,' she said to me once. I can only guess at the anguish she must have felt about both his death and the way of his dying.

As it was, she gave her love unstintingly to other women's children.

When the summer term ended, we all went up to Arthington, though not yet to the big house. I rather dreaded going, but we had a lovely time. I had always adored staying there as a guest, but you view places differently when they belong to you, and it was a novel and entrancing experience. Though I enjoyed much about the school, I never really felt it was a home. Suddenly a future started to seem possible for us. At the end of the holidays Charlie went into the Middlesex for a couple of days for tests. They were clear.

Early in the autumn term we did something we had never done before during the term-time – convalescent holiday excepted. We went away for a weekend. We were both in celebratory mood about Charlie's check-up, and felt we were edging our way back to our original joy in each other's company. We stayed in Suffolk with Charlie's cousin Robin and his wife, Lilias, who were special friends as well as relations.

Nan waved us off, telling us to have a lovely time together, and not to worry about the children. After we'd said goodbye, she suddenly ran after us and gave me an extra goodbye hug, and told me that she wanted me to know that despite all our dramas, she was happier with us than with any other family she'd ever been with. I was extremely touched.

We had a blissful weekend, and there was much laughter. We had decided to go home before lunch on Monday morning, and Lilias brought us our breakfast in bed as a parting treat. I remember feeling particularly happy. We were drinking our coffee and reading the papers when Lilias came into our room, wandered round for a bit and wandered out again. She did this twice without saying anything, and it seemed a bit odd. Then she came back yet again.

'It's no good,' she said. 'I have to make myself tell you. Hang on to each other – but Nan is dead.'

I cannot describe the shock of this announcement. I simply couldn't believe it to start with, and thought Lilias must have got it wrong. It was with a terrible sense of unreality that we hastily packed up and set off home.

Nan had apparently had a massive coronary some time during the night and had been dead for some hours before Belinda, aged six, and quite beside herself with panic, was discovered pummelling and jumping on her, trying to wake her up. Susannah, aged twenty months, was screaming hysterically in her cot. A friend who shared the school run with me had raised the alarm. Not finding Belinda ready at the front door, she had walked through the school and come round to the nursery to see why they were late. It was thought Belinda must have been trying to rouse Nan for nearly a couple of hours. The horror of it is still a vivid memory of Belinda's.

Children's grief is difficult to cope with: it can make them withdrawn, it can make them block something out, or it can make them behave outrageously badly – an understandable cry for help – but it is not always possible to condone extreme naughtiness, and I think children can feel even more insecure if you do. It was hard to get the balance right. While I was writing this book, my daughter Belinda told me for the first time, how she remembers desperately trying to force Nan's hearing aid into her ear while she tried to rouse her. She was convinced this was the reason Nan couldn't hear her. She had never spoken of this before. What anguish locked up inside a child of six! I was horrified that I had somehow failed to release this bit of information at the time. It had lain there, inside her, like a time bomb waiting to explode.

Nan was only fifty-three.

The loss of Nan left a huge gap in our lives. Susannah, who must have heard someone say it before we got back, kept on and on, droning, 'Nan dead, Nan dead,' like a machine that I was unable to switch off. Not surprisingly, Belinda was very much affected. A funny, bright, wilful, highly-strung child, she became extremely difficult for a time.

I now wonder if we should have been more truthful with her. We told her that Nan had suddenly become very ill and was unconscious during the nightmare time when Belinda had been trying to wake her, and that she had then been taken to hospital. We warned her that Nan might not get better, and after two days explained that she had died. At the time I wanted to protect her from the knowledge that she had been battering at a dead body, but I have no idea if this was right.

Nan's funeral was down in Cornwall, and poor Hilda was terribly upset because I didn't attend. There was no way I was prepared to go away, even for one night, at that particular moment and leave my two disturbed and bewildered little girls with anyone else, though I minded hurting Hilda very much. She said the rest of her family would take it as a slight on my part. Though I wrote to them all and tried to explain, Hilda never pretended to understand, and I don't think she ever forgave me, but I knew for absolute certain what Nan herself would have wanted and expected me to do, and I did it.

I grieved for Nan for a long time. A precious friend and a huge support was gone from my life and those of my little girls. If I have learnt any wisdom about dealing with small children, most of it comes from Nan.

Charlie was wonderful. This time there was no need for me to try and disguise my feelings from him and he realized I was near cracking point. Luckily, when there are children involved, it is easier to hold yourself together.

My confidence in the future was again in tatters but, as it happened, the death of Nan ended our four years of disasters.

It was as if someone very strong and special had been loaned to support us through a testing time. When she had dashed after me to tell me how much she loved us, as we departed for our Suffolk weekend, I had absolutely no presentiment that it was a last farewell, but I often wonder if she had some sort of foreknowledge. It had been done with a sort of urgency that was not in character.

I shall always feel privileged that she was part of our family for six years.

This poem was written during that one special week in the year before summer has painted the countryside a uniform colour, when each tree seems a different shade of green and the leaves dance to the tune of spring. It never fails to lift my heart and blow low spirits away.

Wearing Green

The wind is wearing green today
to shimmy through the beech trees,
breaking a two-four rhythm up
– shaking with ragtime gladness:

it kicks its heels high in the spring
and charlestons through the leaves of May.

Dance in my heart again, green wind,
to blow the pain of loss away
and syncopate my sadness.

Borrowed Time

We live on a very expensive loan.
Sometimes I wonder whether
we can keep the payment up:
the question swings, a pendulum, between us.
We hear its slow insistent tick
but do not talk of it.

Once we swigged laughter together,
a bubbly intoxicating brew
that has become too strong for you;
now we share quiet amusement
a soft still drink
but not without danger.

We no longer dance
but the room is wreathed in Verdi.
Eyelids pulled by a single string
spring to release a glance
that flies between us
on a special note;
simultaneously, individual axes
fell a stubborn crossword clue

– and I forget our mortgage rate.

Part Three

After this turbulent period, it took time to build up the confidence to believe that life could ever again flow along without hidden whirlpools and undertows waiting to drag us all under, but gradually, as the months rolled on and no new disasters occurred, optimism grew.

When our spell of ill-luck had started, I was very young and, in the early days of marriage to someone so much older than me, I had often felt out of step with my contemporaries, lacking close friends whose lives in any way resembled mine, and consequently I felt rather lonely. Now I had acquired a lot of new friends of varying ages and lifestyles. Some of them had troubles too, and I learnt that often the people whom to start with one envies have hidden problems and sadnesses to cope with that are not apparent on first meeting. I had grown up. The parents of boys in the school no longer seemed a different generation and many became my close friends as well as Charlie's. An advantage of the big age gap has been that I never think much about anyone's age now – even my own – and like, or don't like, people for themselves rather than because they are contemporaries. I feel lucky to have friends of all ages and from very varying walks of life, and this has enriched my life. I would dread being in any particular clique. All these changes helped me through this difficult time. These troubles gave me a tremendous sense of thankfulness for the good times of life and have been a useful yardstick for deciding what is important and for ordering priorities.

We achieved another baby, this time our son, William, and I could hardly believe my good fortune.

We made our defiant gesture at fate and moved into the big house at Arthington. It may not have been an inspired financial decision – we were never much good at those – and comparisons to living on the Forth Bridge spring to mind, but we never regretted it and had some brilliantly happy years there. No one can take those away.

Arthington is blessed with two remarkable features: a stunning view up the river Wharfe and an extraordinary flyover staircase designed in 1801 by the great Yorkshire architect John Carr, who revamped a much older house that had been partially burned down some years earlier.

The hospital had put props under the sixteen unsupported treads of the flyover and boarded in the elegant banisters. It was a thrilling moment when we took all this camouflage away and ran up the centre flight, which bounced like a trampoline just as Charlie had always told me it would. The stairs took some fearful punishment over the ensuing years as our children and their friends thundered up and down.

We renovated rooms gradually. The first thing that happened when we turned on the ancient central heating to dry the house out was that mould sprang out over the walls like a measles rash. It looked as if someone had taken a brush and flicked black paint everywhere. Harry Pennington, or Pen as he was always called, who had been the handyman for more years than anyone could remember, became my great ally and teacher. We both had a love affair with the house.

Under his instruction I became a dab hand at wallpapering, though my first effort was a disaster. Always one to act first and read instructions later, I had nipped up a ladder with a sixteen-foot drop of paper to which I had liberally applied glue, without the faintest idea of the right way to go about it. Luckily Pen heard my shrieks and rescued me, entirely wound around with paper and glue, bound as tightly as Lazarus in his grave clothes, and rapidly being turned into an interesting papier-mâché sculpture.

An unreliable roof became part of my life. One particular trouble spot was a bow window: on its moulded ceiling a naked nymph stood elegantly surrounded by a garland; overhead was a treacherously porous leaded balcony. I shall never forget the surprise on the faces of members of an architectural society to whom I was giving a conducted tour, when one of my small daughters rushed in to announce in thrilling accents, 'Come quickly, Mummy! That lady in the drawing-room has started leaking all over the floor again.'

At the time of their death, my in-laws had three full-time gardeners, one of whom now retired, leaving Harry Ward, the head gardener, and Jim, who helped him.

Harry was one of the most delightful people I have ever known, and one of the very few who was totally content with his life without being the least bit smug. Harry had started as a garden-boy at Arthington aged fourteen. He was musical and had sung in the church choir as a child. After he started work, he remembered hoping to be set to weed the flower beds outside the library window, so that he could listen to Charlie's grandfather playing the organ. I never heard Harry speak ill of anyone, or anyone of him, but he was far from dull, with a dry sense of humour and a nice turn of phrase.

He and Charlie had played much village cricket together and were already best mates.

The gardens had always been immaculately kept, but neither of my in-laws had wanted to make changes, so there was plenty of scope for new ideas. Harry and Charlie now proceeded to garden in total harmony, each admiring the knowledge and expertise of the other. Between them, they made something wonderful of the six and a half acres of garden. In winter they could occasionally be seen sneaking off together across the park, like a couple of truant boys, for an armed foray to pot a pheasant.

Harry was methodical and pin-neat; Charlie, ferociously untidy. There was a famous occasion when Charlie, who was on the Northern Horticultural Society's council, took Harry to the big annual Flower Show at Harrogate. Harry, immaculate in suit and tie, with the 'Member's Guest' badge pinned to his lapel, sailed through the turnstile, but Charlie, straight off the herbaceous border in his old gardening clothes, was stopped.

'Where did you get that badge? Those badges are not transferable,' said the official at the gate, tapping Charlie's Vice-President's badge with an accusing finger. It took the intervention of a fellow council member before Charlie was allowed in. Harry and Charlie both enjoyed this episode enormously.

Harry was the authority on vegetables, pot plants and the fabulous grapes, peaches and melons that grew in the greenhouses; Charlie was the authority on trees, shrubs and the rhododendron family, and was in charge of layout and new schemes; together they shared the care of the spectacular long herbaceous border. They had the greenest fingers imaginable.

In a book on gardens open to the public, a well-known gardening writer described Charlie's style as highly idiosyncratic. That was about right. He adored colour, the brighter the better, and held the theory, which I partly go along with, that nothing in nature can clash. He loved growing things – if they were not supposed to do well in our soil or climate, but he could make them flourish, so much the better. If he liked a plant, he would bung it in – somewhere. Arthington was not the garden for purists who only like restraint and architectural lines. It was stuffed with interesting species, and at its best was sensational – but not for the faint-hearted.

I like to think that both house and garden gave a good deal of pleasure to many people – and raised a lot of money for various charities into the bargain.

After a few years of spending term-time at the school and holidays at Arthington, we decided to move north full time. Our successors for taking on the school had been lined up for a long time and were ready to do so, and, after so much serious illness, we felt it might be good for Charlie to settle back in his beloved Yorkshire in a less demanding job. It was a difficult decision, but proved to be a good one. I had been afraid that Charlie, a truly vocational schoolmaster, might miss the school terribly. He, I think, had some anxiety as to whether he would feel a loss of identity. We need neither of us have worried. We both took to Yorkshire life immediately.

Some halcyon years followed. I adored Arthington. The house was usually full of friends and relations of all generations, and throbbed with life. Some people find their children's teenage years specially trying, but I loved this time – which is not to say that any of our children were special paragons of virtue, just that I found them enormous fun and their ideas fascinating. They are three strong, but very different, characters who have remained exceptionally close. As they became more independent, and the parental role modified, I marvelled at the pleasure of real friendship with them, and loved having all their friends to stay.

Charlie and I both got involved with local affairs. We made a lot of wonderful new friends and he resumed some old friendships started in his youth.

Gradually the threat of cancer receded, though anxiety crouched like a watchdog, one eye half open, at the back of my consciousness.

A year before our silver wedding anniversary, Charlie succumbed to a nasty virus and took a long time to shake it off. During his two-month convalescence, I was working on a large needlepoint rug to go in front of the fireplace in the drawing-room. It was of white flowers on a black background with borders in two shades of green, and, so that the whole thing was not too unwieldy, I was making it in different squares which could later be joined together. I had designed it, and was pleased with myself. Aunt Evelyn had originally introduced me to canvas work when I was pregnant with Belinda and, in a dilettante way, I had made small cushions and chair seats off and on ever since. There had also been patchwork crazes and a lampshade period, but only when I had people to chat to – reading a book always won if I was on my own. The rug, however, was a big project.

To my utter astonishment, Charlie now asked if I would teach him to sew, so that he could help me. I didn't want my work of art to be botched, and didn't really want to be helped anyway, but I agreed to try. I was sure the idea wouldn't last. Charlie sew? My imagination boggled and I couldn't take it seriously. The family roared with laughter. How wrong we were.

The first week of tuition drove me dotty. There were constant shouts of, 'Darling, could you come here a minute?' 'I can't thread this bloody needle.' 'I've got in a muddle.' 'I can't unravel this bit.' And so on. My heart sank, but I hadn't reckoned with his competitive streak: if Charlie did something, he always had to do it well, preferably better than anyone else. I grudgingly allowed him a square of rug to work on. He thought my tasteful white flowers pretty deadly, but the project raced along much faster than if I'd pottered on by myself. Quite soon he was totally hooked, and started getting bossy about the whole thing.

This new passion of Charlie's gave me a brilliant idea for a silver-wedding present for him. As things turned out, it was undoubtedly the best idea I've ever had. It was to prove our salvation over the coming years.

I asked a friend, the artist Graham Rust, who had painted wonderful murals for us in the house some years before, to design an Arthington tapestry for Charlie and me to make together. At Graham's suggestion I made a list of the things Charlie most loved about the place, and Graham's design included all of them. We had originally thought of a wall-hanging, but in the end it was a screen of four panels, each measuring six foot by two foot. The design was loosely based on Jan Brueghel's *Garden of Eden* in the Victoria and Albert Museum, and was an 'all seasons' representation. It depicted the plants and fruit Charlie grew in the garden and the birds we saw in it; there was a golden retriever and a shih-tzu, honoured representatives of other ones we'd owned; it had snowdrops and roses, melons and onions, spring trees and bare winter branches; it showed pheasants and grouse, goldfinches, kingfishers and Canada geese; and, of course, a sheep to represent the family crest. It depicted the view from the house, the famous 'Belt Walk' of beeches above the river Wharfe, and Alme's Cliff Crag, a local landmark that can be seen from miles around. Graham produced a beautiful water-colour of the design for me to give Charlie on the great day, and meanwhile, with the help of the Women's Home Industries, I had found Miranda Scott, who would paint the whole thing on to canvas from blown-up photographs.

We managed to keep it a complete secret.

That autumn of 1977, to everyone's delight, Belinda married Charles Cox, whom we all adored. Arthington was *en fête* for their wedding.

The following March, a few weeks before our silver wedding, Charlie had a major coronary, and I was once again chasing an ambulance. This time I was lucky enough to have a companion, because Susannah was at home. The day before, she had come down to breakfast white-faced: she'd had a nightmare – a warning dream about disaster for her father. Naturally we didn't tell him, but then neither of us gave it credence that morning either. The next night Charlie woke in the small hours, complaining of pains in the back. He said he thought he might have pulled a muscle moving a shrub, but it soon became obvious that something was seriously wrong as the pain grew really severe, he was sick and in a cold sweat and only half conscious, and I sent for the doctor.

Charlie was in the intensive-care unit of our local hospital for a week, and was then moved to a single room. This was when we first discussed his cancer. Now there was openness, between both us and the doctors; it was a huge relief – I hate being devious. All the same, I was so convinced that optimism had played its part in his recovery before, that I was determined to use this weapon again, and not let him guess how frightened I felt.

Charlie had always been such a physical person: though he loved music – opera was a mutual passion – and enjoyed reading, we could none of us imagine him inactive for long. He had been an outstanding athlete – a double blue at Cambridge, a good golfer and cricketer, and was still a wily tennis player and a good shot. Skiing was easily his favourite sport, and the one we most enjoyed together, but gardening was his most important occupation: not just directing or supervising, but real hands-on gardening of the most energetic kind.

I asked the heart specialist how much Charlie would be able to do if he recovered now.

'It depends what sort of wife you are,' he said. 'Do you believe in quality or quantity?'

'Quality, every time.' I had no doubts about that.

'Then after proper convalescence, I suggest you try, within reason, to let him do what he likes. He strikes me as someone who would be even more stressed by restrictions than by physical activities that will be risky.' I felt immediately that he was right, though I underestimated Charlie's inner resources.

Our marriage had its ups and downs, as all marriages do, but we had more than survived them. I had not been pleased with my own resentful and self-pitying reactions to Charlie's major illness all those years before. I had been in love with him then, but he was infinitely more precious now, and we were very close. I made a vow that if he recovered and I was given a second chance, this time I would play my part better. I think I did, though had I known what a long haul was in front of us, my courage might have failed.

Charlie was desperate to be allowed home for our silver wedding. We had planned a party and a family gathering. We cancelled the party, but decided to keep the family gathering for the weekend. After much nagging, the doctors reluctantly agreed to let him come home earlier than they intended, the day before the great day itself, on condition that he was carried straight upstairs and remained on the same floor for the next eight weeks. They didn't know that on the night of our anniversary, our son, William, my brother, David, and our new son-in-law, put him in a chair and carried him down the perilously swaying Arthington staircase again, to be present at dinner. Charlie was enchanted, and they all laughed so much they nearly dropped him. He was exhausted, but triumphant.

During the eight weeks he was confined upstairs, Charlie started on the first panel of the screen. It became his major occupation.

We decided it would be dull only to use point. We wanted to give the tapestry texture, and more of a three-dimensional effect. I was lucky to find an expert embroidery teacher, Mary Hancock, living in Harrogate. She came and gave Charlie lessons on all sorts of different stitches, and was full of ideas. She also taught me to do long-and-short stitch, or crewel-work, so that I could pick out small details that we wanted to highlight, in either silk or wool.

I shall never give anyone a more successful present than the design for that screen. It was to have a tremendous effect on our lives. His stitchery was undoubtedly one of the factors that kept Charlie going, against all odds, for so long. Our family called it 'Dad's indoor gardening'.

Charlie made a good recovery from that first coronary,

and gradually fought his way back, for a while, to many of his former activities, though not to skiing. I never had the heart to go without him after this. We had other lovely holidays though, notably in Corfu with our children and children-in-law. I was put off going on holiday *à deux* after Charlie had a second coronary when we were on our own in Jamaica. It wasn't as bad as the first, but it was an alarming experience so far from home and with strange doctors. I felt very panic stricken. We had to stay out there longer than planned and our medical insurance paid for us to fly home first class. I had never travelled in such luxury before, and doubt if I ever will again, but despite the miserable reason for it, I have to say we relished that flight.

We still had some more good years left to us, though they were punctuated by alarming health crises, and not a few sadnesses.

Fighting ill-health takes a lot of energy and this is often reflected by a loss, or lessening, of libido. In our early married years, just before and during the time when cancer hit Charlie, I had found nearly three years of sexual abstinence difficult to cope with. It had eroded my self-esteem and fuelled the resentment I felt about his illness. Then I had only been in my twenties; now I was older, wiser and perhaps a little kinder and I coped with it better – but it was still not easy for either of us, especially because Charlie could not bear to talk about it.

Two years after Belinda's wedding, Susannah married Robert Tamworth. We had another Arthington wedding and gained another much-loved and highly congenial son-in-law. William usually had a girlfriend in tow. Grandchildren started to arrive, which was a huge joy to us both, and they often came to stay. Charlie had always been a Pied Piper to small children, and was in his element with them. However, the whole family shared the heartbreak of Belinda and Charles, whose second child, James, was handicapped. We all watched with anguished admiration their struggles on his behalf, especially during his first two years, when he fought for life through crisis after crisis. His life force must be exceptionally strong to have survived. It was a harrowing time.

This is not the place to tell James's story. It deserves a book of its own, which one day I hope Belinda will write. It suffices to say here that James is still very much with us, in many ways a joy and a triumph, but an ongoing difficulty too. Like Nan, he has taught us all a great deal about unconditional love. I found myself grateful for the experience I'd had with Amanda, because it gave me much greater understanding of what Belinda was going through. Though she has gone much further down that particular dark road than I did, it made a special bond between us. It was a consolation to me to be able to put those months of misery from so long ago to such good use now in helping Belinda and to be a 'listening ear' for her. I have to say she was infinitely more generous in sharing her troubles with me than I had been with my mother. No one knows what the cause of James's problems is and to date his condition has no label. There is far more advice available for parents of handicapped children now, and many things had changed in the years between Amanda's birth and James's arrival, but Belinda and Charles have suffered their own share of 'interesting case' experiences too.

My parents came to live at Arthington. Their house in Wales was isolated, their support system had packed up, and my father had been seriously ill with an aneurysm in the head. My brother lived in Scotland; I lived in Yorkshire. Neither of us was exactly on the spot. When one of the two flats we let in the house suddenly became vacant, we tentatively offered it to my mother and father. We were surprised, but relieved, when they accepted. It was a terrible wrench for them to leave Wales, but on the whole it was a good decision for us all. My father had one fairly happy year with us before cancer of the spine got a grip.

I had always adored my father, a funny, special man with an original turn of mind which was sometimes at war with his admiration for convention. He had an offbeat sense of the ridiculous, a quirky way of looking at things and great charm. It was painful to watch him deteriorate, and to witness his mental and physical anguish. He had always been a staunch Christian and a great churchgoer. It saddened me that this faith now seemed to bring him so little comfort. He, who had led such an upright life, who had been a dedicated and much-loved schoolmaster, and perhaps the most courteous person I shall ever know, now became obsessed with what he considered to be his own sinfulness. Judged by less exacting standards, they seemed such very little sins, no more, often less, than the small indulgences and selfishness to which we all succumb. I like to think that just by listening to him I brought him some comfort, but it was deeply distressing. Charlie, who had always been particularly fond of my father and admired him in many ways, sometimes resented the toll this took on me. It was a sad and difficult time for my mother.

My mother had always been strong on backbone and weak on antennae. She was a very gutsy lady, the least self-pitying person in the world, and a great character. She was capable of enormous generosity and unselfishness, but could be both jealous and possessive, and sometimes breathtakingly unkind, for which she would afterwards be sorry. She could also be great fun, with a good, though not particularly subtle, sense of humour, and had the endearing quality of being able to laugh at herself. Unlike my father, she was totally practical – a doer. She had been blessed with tremendous physical energy herself, and did not always understand the limitations of lesser mortals. She loved to minister to her family, in sickness or in health, but she liked to be in charge and expected good results, and my father was on an irreversible decline. She would undoubtedly have died for him, but his increasing slowness irritated her to distraction. She had always been notoriously difficult to help: like the Little Red Hen of children's literature, she preferred to do everything herself. I felt for her deeply, but while there was great love between us, we were not always good at giving each other the right comfort or support. With the best intentions on both sides, we often missed each other's target.

My brother, David, came to visit as often as he could, and was always able to lift my father's spirits for a short time, as those of us who saw him every day could not. These two very different characters must have had one of the best father–son friendships ever, compounded of shared interests, especially sporting ones, and great mutual admiration – a lovely, rare relationship. We managed to keep my father at home with the help of night nurses. At the end he became so thin and frail he seemed almost transparent.

He lived nearly a year after his doctors told me that he probably had about three weeks left. One night, when I went to say goodnight to him, he suddenly said to me: 'I've decided it's not worth going on. I'm not as David would want me to be.'

I would have liked to stay and hold his hand that night, but knew my mother wouldn't like it. I was not surprised when, two hours later, she came through to our side of the house, and knocked on our bedroom door to say, 'Pa's gone.'

I tried to put my feelings for my father into a poem, 'Time to Straighten Your Tie'. It was written with love and admiration, but sadly, at the time when it was first published, my mother didn't like it and thought it critical. I have always felt badly about this. It is some comfort that she rather came round to the poem later.

I found it hard, after he died, to get my father back in my mind as the delightful companion of so much of my life. The pathetic, sick, and occasionally querulous, old man of the last years kept intruding. I think this is a common, but distressing, part of mourning for someone who has gradually declined.

Two years after my father died, I had a curious, but comforting experience. We had not been talking about him, nor had he been specially in my mind, but one night I had an extraordinarily vivid dream about him. I dreamt that we met in the courtyard outside my grandparents' house, where all family arrivals and departures took place. I could see my father coming from a long way off, first as a light, then as a recognizable person. We zoomed in towards each other like two shooting stars from space. He looked radiant, his very blue eyes full of laughter, and immediately brought back for me my childhood vision of him. I could smell his particular, clean, tweedy and slightly tobaccoey smell. (I'd forgotten that when I was a small child he had smoked a pipe.) We did not speak: there was no need. We exchanged a long embrace – a much deeper one than we had ever done in life. My father, always physically inhibited about expressing affection, was not a huggy person. We gazed into each other's eyes and I knew he was all right. Then we whooshed away from each other and I woke up filled with happiness. I lay in bed, savouring the moment – and then I realized that I could still smell tobacco smoke. I couldn't believe it, and thought there must be some real source, an intruder perhaps, which was an alarming idea. Charlie was fast asleep beside me. I got up and went into our bathroom next door and turned on the light. Not only could I still smell the pipe smoke, but I could now see it. It wreathed all round me. There was absolutely no mistaking it and I was stunned. It must have lasted for about five minutes, and then it suddenly vanished as completely as if a television set had been switched off. I went downstairs immediately and wrote the experience down, lest I should doubt my own memory in the morning.

When I told my brother about this, he said, 'Of course. Players Gold Block tobacco.'

I am aware that different people will have different explanations for this incident. I can only say that for me it was both real and profoundly consoling. Charlie, who had a strong belief in the survival of the spirit and the paranormal, though he could be persuaded only occasionally to discuss it, totally accepted this as evidence of my father's survival.

We all trembled for how my mother, always so deeply wrapped up in her family, would cope without someone to look after. She was remarkable. I never saw her shed a tear, though she may have done so in private. Life appeared to go on as usual: she still stuck to her domestic routine and there was no lessening of standards. I am not implying, not for one moment, that she didn't miss my father terribly. I am sure she did, but there was certainly no outward display or question of collapse.

No one could possibly have wanted my father to struggle on, and I was so deeply aware that the same thing might happen to Charlie at any time that I was constantly braced for disaster, in itself an exhausting state. My mourning for my father became part of my sadness for Charlie. I find it hard in retrospect to separate them.

The house and garden were starting to show ominous signs of deterioration – all the outbuildings and glasshouses were collapsing – and a complete rethink was required, but Charlie no longer had the energy or the will to take decisions. I sometimes felt surrounded, as in the hymn 'Abide with Me', by 'change and decay in all around I see'. It is not actually change but decay that is so depressing to live with. I often felt as though I walked about with a secret rock in my heart.

Because I slept badly, sometimes in the spring and summer I would get up very early, as light was breaking, to walk by the river with my dogs. Some mornings the river would be covered in mist so that only the tops of trees could be seen, giving it the ethereal look of a Chinese painting. Occasionally I would be lucky enough to watch a kingfisher having its breakfast on the opposite bank, balancing a small fish sideways across its beak and then tossing it up, like a pancake, to slither head first down its throat. I would watch the sun come up and balance on the edge of my world like a ball of fire, and the garden would be alive with the activity of small animals and birds, and full of wonderful fresh smells. In the woods behind the house I might see hares and rabbits, roe-deer and occasionally a fox – though I always kept quiet about this. All this was my comfort.

Perhaps I did not let my grief out enough. I was so afraid that if I let go, I might fall apart, but writing poetry was a secret solace, a way of getting things off my chest without upsetting anyone else. I recommend it.

*

There were still lots of bright spots: many kind friends; a home and surroundings we loved; many wonderful visits from our family and the growing band of grandchildren, who were a joy. Charlie had not entirely lost his capacity to be brilliantly funny at times (something our son has inherited), and we loved each other's company, but he seemed to be fading, like a bright water-colour that has been exposed to too much light.

Arthington has its own water supply. Once it had supplied the farms on the estate and all the village: now there were only a few houses beside ourselves still dependent on it. We were always having water crises – usually at bank holidays or when the house was particularly full. This was not due to the spring that supplied the little reservoir at the top of the hill; even in famously dry summers that never dried up completely. The trouble came from the complicated network of ancient pipes, which was always bursting underground. As fast as we located and dealt with one trouble spot, another would occur, and the whole process of search and patch up would begin again. It was horrendously expensive.

I began to feel there was a strong similarity with Charlie. His life force was amazingly strong, but his system was beginning to pack up. It would be boring to list all his health problems – there were so many. It is enough to say that he was nearly always in discomfort, often in pain. He had a degenerative neuropathy and his legs in particular became very painful: walking any distance was a matter of will-power. Polymyalgia rheumatica was controlled by the steroids on which he was to remain for the rest of his life. The dosage of all the pills which he had to take was a constant juggling act. His drive came from within and not from a surplus supply of energy, which was at a premium. He was extraordinarily uncomplaining. This period was expensive for us both: he would push himself to the limit, and sometimes I could hardly bear to watch.

When Harry Ward retired, after fifty-five years with the family, Charlie insisted on wobbling up ladders to prune the vines. We still had Jim, but only part time. On his own admission Jim was no expert, nor one to take any initiative. He was a wonderful digger and tidier-up but he was no longer young either.

The screen had become Charlie's pride and passion, and provided him with a wonderful alternative occupation when he couldn't garden. He became much more expert than I was, and was far more dedicated. He would sit and stitch away for hours, listening to music – often Wagner – played full pitch. Because it was such fine work, it was a worrying moment when we discovered that a split retina in his left eye was not repairable. For two bad months his right eye was out of action too, after a thrombosis, and I was terrified he was going blind. Mercifully that cleared up.

It was a hugely exciting moment when the screen was finished, and we were very honoured to be asked to lend it for an exhibition in London, at Sotheby's, as part of a joint venture with the Royal Horticultural Society, called the Glory of the Garden. It was on show for a month and even got a special mention from Roy Strong on the radio. Sotheby's and the RHS threw a special preview party, a Lenders' Luncheon. Charlie had already started to find social gatherings too exhausting, and didn't think he could cope with this one. He hadn't been away for ages either, but I felt this was his moment of glory, as it was very largely his work. Somehow he made it. I've always been thankful that, for once, I really pressured him to go. He adored it, and we had a lovely day. It was the last time he went to London.

It had become difficult for me to go away, even for a couple of nights. Charlie, who had been the least possessive of husbands and always encouraged me to follow my own interests, had now become very dependent on me. I hated to leave him, and he hated having anyone else to look after him; he wouldn't admit this was necessary but he could no longer cope alone.

I felt in a sort of limbo, suspended in time, dreading what I knew must come, feeling far away from the happy times we'd had, but sometimes finding it difficult to enjoy the many blessings that were still left to us. I never knew what was going to happen next. It was a real lesson in trying to live 'in the now', as the jargon phrase has it. I suppose I had already started my grieving process for Charlie. It is hard to watch someone you love suffer and deteriorate, and know that life is not going to get better for them.

There were times when the quality I had said I so firmly believed in for him didn't seem good enough, and yet there were still many moments when we shared great happiness together. The poem at the start of this section tries to express my feelings about this period of our life.

Then Charlie had a stroke. To start with, he was completely paralysed down the right side. His speech came and went, and was very blurred, though he was absolutely on the button mentally. With the help of a nurse who came for an hour, morning and evening, I managed to keep him at home. One of the therapies was to put a squash ball in his right hand and fold his fingers round it; he was supposed to try and squeeze it. He couldn't even feel it, and found this very depressing. Then a healer friend of mine gave us a suggestion that proved to be a turning point. She told me to tell Charlie to make a picture in his mind of a whole lot of telephone lines that were 'down' or out of order, but to concentrate on the fact that there were also plenty of spare lines along which messages could be passed. Charlie looked scornful when I put this idea to him, but it was typical of him that he secretly tried it – and persevered.

I had long had an interest in healing and, in particular, in the bringing together of orthodox medicine with healing and alternative therapies, and I belonged to a doctors' and healers' network. Charlie had always regarded my activities in this area with amused, but tolerant, interest. Luckily our wonderful group of GPs, a teaching practice, were not against some of my 'cranky' ideas, and indeed have a healer at their surgery one day a week. Visualization is now regarded in many hospitals as a valuable tool in the fight against cancer. Anyway, Charlie felt afterwards that this mental exercise had a profound effect on his recovery. He had formidable powers of concentration, and if he took something up, there were never half measures.

Soon after this, he indicated to me that I should turn back the blankets of our bed. There was a slight, but perceptible, movement in his big toe. We gazed at each other in delight.

Having read about experiments carried out in the States testing 'energy levels' before and after healers held their hands over water – with fascinating, positive results – and wishing to make my own contribution to Charlie's healing, I had got into the habit, when running his bath before the nurse arrived in the morning, of secretly having a little charging-up session over the bath water. I felt pretty silly, but at least no one could see, and it could certainly do no harm. While taking it seriously on one level, I also thought it was pretty funny myself, and rashly told Susannah and William, who had come to visit their father. They wailed with laughter and said, 'Watch old Mum charging up the Holy Water' every time I put a slug of Fairy Liquid in the washing-up bowl. All the same, they were not entirely sceptical. I haven't the faintest idea whether my efforts were helpful, but at least it gave me something to do. I never told Charlie about this latest eccentricity of mine.

For whatever reason, Charlie now proceeded to improve. After eight weeks his speech was back, only becoming slurred if he was tired, he could walk a few steps with someone holding him on his bad side, and squeeze the squash ball. As soon as he could do this, I decided it would be just as good therapy, and far more fun, if he could try and sew again. I bought a square of large-hole rug canvas, a huge bodkin and some thick wool, threaded it up and said, 'Get practising.' At the same time, by chance, I found two brilliant books on Bargello needlepoint, with all sorts of ideas for adapting patterns into four triangles to make squares. The patterns were complicated to work out and I knew they would appeal to the mathematician in Charlie. A whole new era of cushion making began. I have beside me now the first 'therapy' cushion he made after his stroke. He made far better ones later, and got back to finer canvas, but this one is infinitely precious to me – a testament to his courage.

I also decided that if I could only get him out to the garden, he would start to improve even more. Because by now it was August, a lot of wheelchairs had apparently been hired or borrowed for people to take on holiday, but I managed to find one in the end, though it was a ropy old contraption. As in many north-of-England country houses, the gardens were some little way from the house. It was hard work pushing Charlie up the steep hill to get to the herbaceous border and the two walled gardens, and I could only just manage it, tacking diagonally and puffing like a pressure cooker – good for the calf muscles. Coming back was another matter. Because the chair had only a parking break and I wasn't strong enough to hold it back, we used to come hurtling downhill, full tilt, with me running flat out. There was no way of stopping until we gradually came to a halt. I used to pray a car wouldn't suddenly come up the drive. Charlie said it was the most exciting thing he'd done since skiing, and looked forward to this thrill in his restricted life. I can't say I did.

However, apart from this bright moment of danger in our day, Charlie hated the wheelchair. I miscalculated when I thought it would cheer him up to be pushed round outside, because he only longed to be able to garden himself. It made him grumpy and critical to Jim – though never to me – about the work he was doing, and I would feel ashamed of such curmudgeonly behaviour. When I was researching other people's experiences for this book, a more recently widowed friend told me how hurt and surprised she had been when her adored husband, who died much too young of leukaemia, became cross and resentful to her when she pushed him in a wheelchair. In our case, I suppose Jim acted as a whipping boy for me. Perhaps it was stupid and insensitive of me not to have foreseen this effect of frustration.

The next idea I had was much better.

It was actually some time since Charlie had driven a car, though he liked to keep up the fiction that he could if he wanted to, but now it was obvious he would never do so again. Eventually he got back to being able to walk short distances unaided, and I hit on the notion that it would be a much better idea to sell his BMW and buy an electric buggy so that he could get himself round the gardens. I knew he hated being dependent on me. As a surprise I arranged for a firm in Leeds specializing in gadgets for the disabled to bring three out for us to try. Susannah brought her children from Derbyshire for the day to add to the jollity of the occasion.

The cheapest model, which I knew would be the one that Charlie, a thriftier character than me, would go for, was a three-wheeler; it was also the least stable, and I was certain it would be in for some exciting driving. I think these buggies are really designed for sedate pavement use, but ours would be roaring through rough grass and speeding over earth and gravel. The helpful man from the shop sportingly agreed to let me try it out in front of Charlie, corner it too sharply, and deliberately overturn in it. The buggy we eventually bought, a four-wheeler, was brilliant. Susannah's children were utterly enchanted and made Charlie feel that, far from an invalid carriage, he had a magic chariot. Rides in it became hugely coveted by all the grandchildren.

This was to provide Charlie with gardening legs. The buggy had two speeds: fast and slow. Charlie always drove it on fast. Luckily it bleeped in reverse and our dogs learnt to leap smartly out of the way when they heard the sound. Yum-Yum, the shih-tzu of the time and Charlie's inseparable companion, used to ride about with him wherever he went. Charlie's family had always had golden retrievers – we still do – but we acquired our first shih-tzu just after we were married. Charlie wanted to give me a crocodile bag for my birthday – very much the smart thing at the time and even then hideously expensive. He gave me a cheque and sent me up to London to choose one. I came back with an eight-week-old shih-tzu puppy instead. I've never had, or wanted, a crocodile bag, but I've had shih-tzus ever since: much better value.

Some quality returned to our life. Charlie could buggy off independently and pot things up in the greenhouse, and astonishingly, made himself sew again – and well, too – though it was an effort. Everything was an effort. He made rugs and cushions for all the family. I dreaded him finishing any project, and felt under terrific pressure to come up with new ideas of things for him to make. It was the opposite of Penelope unravelling work in the hope of Ulysses' return.

Occupations can be vital – literally – to invalids, but tact is required in suggesting them. The last thing you want is to emphasize their failing faculties or make them feel their inactivity is a burden, so ingenuity is called for both in thinking up projects within their physical range and then in presenting the idea. Sometimes my imagination was taxed to the limit. No doubt Charlie sometimes found my efforts maddening, though he never let on. It was a rather desperate charade we played with each other. I found the most successful approach was 'Wouldn't it be fun if we could do so-and-so?' and then let Charlie's natural team-leader tendency take over so that the project became his.

I rarely showed my poems to Charlie, who greatly encouraged me to write, was delighted when I got any of them published, but didn't much care for the results, except for the satirical or humorous ones, which amused him. Here is one I wrote for one of our last wedding anniversaries, which he did like. I had wanted to try to find some way of expressing my admiration for his courage – and my love. I know he was pleased.

At Needlepoint

For C. E. W. S.

You hold your life
Together with stitches;
Force frayed thread
Through the narrowing eye
Of each day's sharp needle
And ward off death
With a bodkin.

Once you climbed mountains
Hit boundaries served aces;
Planted avenues of poplars
Nurtured Loderi St George
And grew exotic fruit.
You pruned trees from the top
Of a tall ladder.

Now with great effort
You dig embroidered gardens
And labour in herbaceous
Needlepoint. Each vanquished row
Is the end of a tournament
And you ski down your precipice
On a strand of wool.

They are very beautiful
These new flowers you grow;
You still use green fingers
But cultivate strange plants
In an unlikely climate
And nothing can unravel
The tapestry of our love.

With his stroke, Charlie, who had enjoyed good food and been something of a connoisseur of wine, lost his sense of taste. Worse, he had a filthy taste in his mouth, so food and drink were actually unpleasant. Meals became a nightmare.

As the degenerative nerve disease progressed, he found it hard to swallow and started to have bouts of sudden extreme illness, when he would run a high temperature, become alarmingly distended, have terrific rigors, be sick and sometimes delirious. I think they were called pseudo-intestinal stoppages. Antibiotics usually worked, but sometimes it would involve a dash to hospital. For eighteen months we never went more than six weeks without one of these terrifying episodes.

One particular time when he was rushed into St James's, Leeds, with a temperature of 105, he could only answer questions in needlework terms. It would have been funny if it hadn't been so awful. I knew more or less what he meant but, not surprisingly, the doctors didn't. The surgeon would poke him in the tummy and ask, 'Does this hurt here?' and Charlie would say things like, 'Well, I think the canvas is a little tight there', or 'That hole is too small to get a needle through', or 'No, that's all right – that's a good stitch.'

Recently, while reading a book called *Final Gifts* by two hospice nurses, Maggie Callanan and Patricia Kelley, on the importance of trying to listen to, and understand, the 'coded messages' of the dying, I thought of this episode. Charlie was well aware of all that was going on around him, and afterwards felt outraged that he was treated as if he had no understanding because his speech was muddled. He was doing his best to answer questions which he perfectly understood, but just couldn't use the right idiom.

In between these awful bouts it would be business as usual. In the morning Charlie would sew in bed while listening to music, and I would get him downstairs for lunch. Then, weather permitting, it would be out in the buggy to do what he could in the garden. He was most inventive about this and it was astounding what he still managed to do, dragging himself about and achieving impossible things. He hit on the idea of letting a few people have a patch of garden in which to grow their own things – a sort of allotment – in return for occasional help with other bits of the garden, and this was very useful, but the wilderness was encroaching fast and this measure was not enough to keep it at bay. I was thankful that there were places where even the buggy couldn't go, and which therefore Charlie could not see. As I had expected, the buggy had a rough life.

Sport on television was a welcome distraction, but he found it increasingly difficult to read for any length of time. A subscription to a jigsaw-puzzle library was a brilliant present from my mother. She and Charlie, who were secretly fond of each other, covered it up well and lived in a state of mutual respect for each other's courage – and armed neutrality.

I was getting anxious about how much longer I could

hold out physically, and both our doctor and my children started to put pressure on me to take a proper break. Kind friends offered to come and sleep in, but Charlie would have hated it. He liked seeing those he loved for short visits, but found conversation tiring, and there were other problems. His plumbing had for some time become unreliable and he dreaded the indignity of it. Anyone who has looked after a long-term invalid will know how miserable this can be.

I had made one or two attempts to go away for the odd night, for weddings or special occasions, but it was increasingly difficult, and twice I had to be called back as soon as I arrived at my destination. Charlie, who had always been so unselfish about this and in particular encouraged me to go and stay with his adored daughters, now became resistant. It was a shock when this first became obvious.

Though Belinda and Charles then lived in London, his home was in Scotland. His parents had built themselves a small house and made the bigger house over to Charles and Belinda so that it could once again have a young family in it. Charles was working and I had promised Belinda I would go and spend the first night of the school holidays in Scotland with her and the children. She arrived to spend a night at Arthington to see her father, and I was to drive north with her next day, stay for one night, and then fly home. I had organized someone to hold the fort for me. Charlie, famous for his welcomes to his family, hardly gave her a greeting, and it became clear that he resented her for taking me away.

I cannot describe how out of character this was. We were stunned, and Belinda was deeply upset.

I hate writing this: in view of Charlie's amazing stoicism,

constant love and usual consideration for me, it seems disloyal, but perhaps to admit that it happened will help someone else. When someone you love starts to change, it is a true bereavement: a terrible, terrible loss, almost worse than death itself. Very rarely he would speak to me about his increasing helplessness and despair, and at least then I could try to comfort him. It was his occasional outbursts of frustrated pettiness about unexpected things – never about the big things – that upset us, because it was so out of character. At other times he would be withdrawn. It was like having a really beautiful and expensive garment – a cashmere sweater, say – that has been a special favourite, a much-admired garment for all seasons, but has shrunk and faded so much from too hot a wash that it no longer fits. Those who knew it before can see the quality that was there, but to anyone new it is just an old wreck. This feeling is awful. I couldn't bear people who had not known the real Charlie to meet him on an off day. There is not much to be done except slog on, enjoy the good times that still exist, and keep a sense of humour. It is laugh-or-cry time.

There was never a repeat of this lack of welcome, a sure sign that Charlie must have gone through a private agony of remorse, but it showed how much he hated me going away. Thereafter, this took the form of resistance to, and resentment of, anyone who came to care for him in my absence. It was much easier not to go.

Then I gave myself a fright. I went into Harrogate to do some vital shopping, and was spotted by an acquaintance slumped against the car, trying to summon up energy just to move. Clearly something had to be done. I didn't want to go to friends, however understanding, because I knew I would feel I had to make an effort. The family came up with the suggestion of a health clinic, and Susannah said that if I would go for a week, she could get someone to look after her children and would join me for the last few days. I got a charming Australian nurse for Charlie, hardened my heart, and went to Shrublands in Suffolk. I know it saved me from having a serious breakdown.

After a massage session the first day, I realized I was about to get a cracking migraine – something from which I've always suffered, learnt to cope with, and which was not therefore unusual. However, I had opted for one of the cheaper rooms, in a separate house five minutes' walk from the main building. I knew I must get over there fast to take my pills – but I couldn't make it. I was violently sick, and when one of the staff came to see if I was all right, I started to cry and simply couldn't speak. I could neither explain nor stop. I just went on being sick and crying.

I cannot begin to describe how wonderful everyone at Shrublands was. Someone went to collect my belongings, and I was moved to a room in the main house – as it turned out, at no extra charge – and put to bed. I cried out my grief for the loss of Charlie, both the parts of him I had already lost, and the certain loss of the rest of him which I knew must come. I cried for the deterioration of my beloved home and the decline of a beautiful garden. I cried from exhaustion, from fear – and from the relief of letting go and having a respite. I have shed tears since, mostly in private, but I have never had a great explosion of weeping such as I had then. It was life-saving.

By the time Susannah arrived, I was well on the mend; so much so, that people kept coming up to her to comment on the dramatic change in my appearance. I had apparently arrived looking so like a ghost that even complete strangers had noticed; now I looked human. William had lent me his huge towelling bathrobe, a Pied Piper's patchwork garment in red, blue, green and yellow – he shares his father's love of bright colours – and as I was collecting my diet tray, looking like a stick insect and totally enveloped in this Joseph's dream-coat, a voice behind me said, 'I would like to kick you.' I turned round, surprised, to see an absolutely colossal man in completely identical garb. I had lots of home-made bread and butter, thick soup, cheese, yoghurt and fruit on my tray: he had hot water with a slice of lemon. We must have looked very funny together.

I may say that I'm not going through a stick-insect phase at the moment, nor am I a stranger to occasional misery-eating binges, though these occur more at times of dreary slog than at those of acute distress. I lost nearly a stone the week after my father's death and did the same again when Charlie died. Not a slimming aid I recommend.

Susannah had just discovered she was pregnant with a much-wanted third child, after a miserable miscarriage the previous year, and it was wonderful to be able to celebrate the hope of a new life at this particular time. We had a lovely few days together.

After a week I went home greatly strengthened to cope with the last lap, which was to last, unbelievably, for two more years.

I was lucky. I had the financial resources to have this vital temporary relief. Many do not. I think anyone who badly needs a break but has not got the money should find out about the carer's allowance, which can be helpful in this situation, and various organizations which may help. I would also say that, just occasionally, however heart-rending it is to leave a beloved invalid, you have to harden your heart and get a break. It is better to have a week away than end up in hospital yourself – but it is easier said than done.

All through these difficult times I had huge support not only from our wonderful GP, Geoffrey Hall, who paid regular home visits to Charlie, but also from his partners – two in particular. Because it is a teaching practice, Geoff Hall would sometimes bring a trainee with him. I used to glow with pride as I heard him explaining Charlie's case to a young doctor. 'You are about to meet a very remarkable man,' he would say. After Charlie died, these three doctors all told me how much they had enjoyed coming to see him over the years, and how privileged they had felt to look after him. It meant so much to me.

Geoff won't mind me saying that as well as being a brilliant doctor, he is something of an eccentric himself – a man after Charlie's heart, always tilting at windmills. His partners say they have to go gently with him the week he returns from holiday, as he's usually near to collapse, having run up several mountains with a backpack on, or having fallen off his racing bike.

Charlie's next adventures took him to hospital for eight weeks. He had always only had to look at the sun to go a rich bronze, the sort of colour some women spend fortunes on sunbeds to achieve. Now, he went orange. He had gall stones in his bile duct. These fish proved hard to catch and there were five attempts before one was fully successful. Each session, though vital, took its toll on him.

The staff at Leeds Infirmary were wonderful, but he desperately longed for home. It was another nightmare time. Just when we were beginning to hope that he might be allowed out, the telephone rang as I walked back into the house after a visit. It was Sister. Could I come back at once? Charlie had just had an internal haemorrhage. He had a perforated ulcer and a major operation was inevitable.

Through the skill of the surgeon and his team, and Charlie's own extraordinary hold on life, he came through that operation against all expectations and lived another year.

It always moved me, during this sad last period, how much our grandchildren adored Charlie. It says a lot about his magic that even when he was a sick, chairbound old man, I don't think they ever thought of him like this. I remember vividly, when I was small myself, cringing and not liking having to kiss my own invalid grandfather, but the children used to rush in and hug Charlie with touching enthusiasm right up to the last. I have a poignant photograph of Arabella, our eldest granddaughter then aged eleven, taken only weeks before Charlie died. He was sitting in his buggy, and she ran over to lean against him. Belinda snapped her just as she had spontaneously laid her cheek against his. He certainly made a profound impression on Susannah's eldest son, young William, who still talks about him and refers back to him, and on whom Charlie was obviously a lasting influence. He was only six when Charlie died.

After years of false alarms, I knew for certain that we had really reached the end of the road, when Charlie suddenly said to me, in tones of some surprise, 'This one's got me. I'm not getting better.' I'm glad I didn't give in to the temptation to deny this. It opened the way for us to talk about many things that had hung between us, unsaid.

I asked him if he was afraid. He said no, he wasn't afraid, but he didn't want to leave me. One day he suddenly said, 'I mind so much that I shall never dance with you again.' Charlie had been a sensational dancer, and together we had fancied ourselves no end on the floor, but it must have been ten years since we had danced together when he said this. Because we were so in tune over this, I can't dance well with anyone else, and feel clumsy and fumble-footed.

Charlie told me he knew he was leaving me with a heap of problems, and felt bad about this. He had just not had the energy to face them, but I'd known this for a long time. I asked if there was anything special he wanted me to do. He said no, but that he liked to think of me 'being around at Arthington' the place which meant so much to us both. Again I'm glad I didn't fall for the temptation to give a false promise, which would have made life even more difficult for me afterwards. I said I would like that too, but couldn't guess what the future might hold. We told each other how much we loved one another, but we knew this anyway.

I had promised our three children that, if possible, I would try and let them know when the end was approaching. This I now did, and Geoff Hall confirmed my view. Charlie was in considerable misery, alleviated by drugs, but nothing worked for long. The wonderful Community nurses came in twice a day. Belinda and William managed to come up for a night, but Susannah's baby, Freddie, was ill that particular day and she couldn't leave him.

That evening Charlie suddenly had a brilliant, short reversal to his old self. He was wildly funny and we were all lit up for half an hour. It was like the sudden last flame of a dying fire, when some unburnt bit of wood flares briefly before the whole thing goes out. The three of us who were there will never forget it.

Next morning Charlie, who had not left our bedroom for days, unnervingly wanted to come down. We managed to get him into his favourite chair downstairs. I left Belinda, who did not have to go back till the evening, with him while I drove William to his train. He and Charlie both had tears in their eyes as they said goodbye.

When I got back, Belinda was very agitated. 'Thank God you're back,' she said. 'Dad's now insisting he must go out, and I've been desperate not knowing what to do.' We draped a rug over his dressing-gown, I got his buggy to the front door and somehow we got him on to it and helped him drive it. By a sort of miracle, Harry Ward, now dreadfully lame with arthritis, was in the gardens. It was the first time they'd seen each other for ages. I still think this was quite extraordinary. Belinda and I couldn't believe it, but typically they both behaved as if it was entirely natural. Nothing was said, but we all knew this was Charlie's farewell to his garden.

Susannah was not so lucky with her last visit. I had warned her that Charlie, heavily doped, was drifting in and out of consciousness and just might not know her. But the moment she came into the room he opened his eyes. 'So how's the babe now, then?' he asked. He knew her all the time, but he was wretched and terribly restless. Together she and I moved him from bed to chair and back again most of the day. He had ceased to be able to be comfortable in his body.

During Charlie's last few days I was reading a book called *Closer to the Light* by an American paediatrician, Dr Melvin Morse, about children's near-death experiences. I lay on the bed beside Charlie much of the time, holding his hand, and reading when he was asleep. It was an extraordinary book to be reading at that particular time.

Charlie had once had an 'out of the body' experience himself in the war. He described to me how he had been lying unconscious on the operating table and suddenly was aware that he was floating above himself. He could see his own body below him, with all the doctors and nurses round him, and could see exactly what was going on in all the parts of the room which he could not possibly have seen from a prone position, let alone with his eyes shut under an anaesthetic. Apparently the medical staff were shattered when he could tell them all sorts of details afterwards that it would have been impossible for him to see. Talking about it to me, he always said, 'The difference between that and a dream is that if you dream, however vividly, the moment you wake up you know it was only a dream. This was real and I knew I had not been dreaming.' I couldn't help hoping that while his sad physical body was suffering and lapsing into bouts of unconsciousness, perhaps his etheric body or spirit was floating happily above, looking down at me and feeling free.

An odd little incident occurred. Our current shih-tzu, Peach, successor to Yum-Yum, was two and a half at this time. She had always slept in the kitchen with the big dogs, but four nights before Charlie died she started to howl after I had shut them up. I really mean howl too: not intermittent barking, but real nose-in-the-air continuous yowling-to-the-moon stuff. She had never done anything like this before – nor has she since. It was the last straw to keep going down to let her out; she didn't want to go out anyhow. After three nights of this bizarre behaviour I was at my wits' end. It was Charlie who suggested we should bring her basket up to our bedroom. 'I'm so doped I don't hear her anyway, but at least you might get some rest,' he said. That night she gave me a look as though to say, 'You were very slow to get the message', settled down and never made a sound. The following night Charlie died. She has been sleeping in my room ever since. I am quite certain that Peach knew that Charlie was about to depart.

On Charlie's last day, Geoff Hall came in the morning and arranged for the Community Sister, who had become a real support, to come later to give him another injection, and I agreed to have a private nurse for one night so that I could get some sleep. I was dropping with exhaustion.

For the last hours, Charlie's breathing had become incredibly loud and laboured; he had not recovered consciousness for some hours. The night nurse, June, arrived at 10.30. After I'd shown her where everything was, I went to have a bath before going to spend the night in William's bedroom. She promised she would come for me at any moment during the night. I had no idea whether Charlie could hear or understand me but I explained what I was doing, just in case. Then I kissed him goodnight, and went very quickly to Will's room. I had not even shut the door when June came after me to say Charlie had died. 'Your husband's pulse actually stopped as you kissed him good- night,' she said, 'but I just had to make sure.'

Afterwards, it was a huge comfort to know that after all we'd been through together, I had actually been with him at the end.

I can't remember if I cried. I don't think I did. I felt an overwhelming relief – and a gaping sense of emptiness. It is an exceedingly odd feeling, when an event which you have for so long anticipated, dreaded, yet in some ways hoped for, finally happens.

I know I rang all three of my children, who all said they would come next day. I must have gone over to tell my mother, though I have no recollection of doing so. It is strange what gaps there are: some quite small things are vividly clear, and others a complete blank. I found my memory unreliable for some time after Charlie's death, and I have heard many other people say the same thing. Even after an expected death, you are in shock. It is so final, so irrevocable.

I rang the doctor on duty, who came. He was kind and brisk and said he would ring Geoff Hall in the morning. One thing I remember very clearly: he and June went to do whatever professionals do after someone has died. After he had gone, June and I went back into my bedroom and I was shattered to see the sheet pulled up over Charlie's face. I couldn't bear it. 'Does it have to be like that?' I asked. 'Of course not,' she said. 'Do what feels right to you.' So I turned it back, as if he'd still been sleeping, drew the curtains back so that the April dawn would flood in, and left a light on in case I wanted to go back in during the night. June said she would still spend the night, though she would now be able to sleep, and it was a comfort to feel there was someone else there. She promised she would come and wake me before she left in the morning. She was very sweet. Then Peach and I went back into Will's bedroom. I took two sleeping pills and, to my surprise, I slept till June brought me a cup of tea at six.

I think it is important, whether in hospital or at home, to follow your own instincts and do whatever feels right to you – not to let anyone, family or professionals, take over and tell you how you should behave at a time of death. I spent time alone with Charlie next morning. He seemed miles away – conspicuous by his absence rather than his presence. When I went back to our room, Peach had immediately jumped up on the bed and curled up on top of Charlie, where she remained till we removed her before he was taken away. When Geoff Hall arrived I apologized, thinking dogs on bodies might not be considered suitable by anyone else, but I should have known him better. 'I hope my dogs keep watch for me like that when I die,' he said.

Belinda, Susannah and William each wanted a short time alone with their father, to make their very private and personal farewells. William said he walked round the room saying aloud all the things that he and Charlie had not said to each other in life. It is often so much easier for women to express both emotion and love than for men, though I think this is getting better nowadays.

When the undertakers arrived later that day, we all four went out for a long walk. I could not have borne to see Charlie carried out.

Susannah and Belinda had managed to make arrangements for their older children, but Susannah had to bring her baby with her. It was lovely to have a new life in the house at the time when an old one had just left it.

Susannah's husband, Robert, was in the States on business, and she had to ring him up in his hotel at what was for him six o'clock in the morning. He was devastated, and specially upset not to have been with Sue when it happened. He and Charles were absolutely devoted to Charlie, and no one could have had more wonderful and supportive sons-in-law.

A few months earlier, William, who had given and received his share of heartbreaks over the years, had produced a new girlfriend. Charlie had asked both me and our daughters if we thought this might really be *the* one this time – he liked her so much. I knew it must indeed be serious when Will asked me, with some diffidence, if he could have her to stay for the funeral as a support. 'Bee and Sue have Charles and Robert,' he said. 'It would mean so much to me to have Alice.' It must have been very daunting for her, because she didn't know us at all well, but she never put a foot wrong at this difficult time. She is now my much-loved daughter-in-law. I have always felt glad that Charlie knew her, but deeply sad that he was but a winter shadow of his real self by the time she met him – back to the analogy of the faded garment.

My mother was very good. We tried hard to include her in everything and she made a real effort to keep her loving but controlling instincts within bounds.

After such a long and gallant struggle to cling on to life, I'd had unrealistic and exalted hopes that when he finally capitulated, Charlie's actual death would be easy – a beautiful, moving experience. It was moving all right but it certainly wasn't easy. There are many well-documented cases of the actual moment of death being amazingly peaceful; of the dying person appearing to see someone who has come to collect them, and reaching out their arms; even of the people at the bedside witnessing the spirit departing from the body attached only by the silver cord, the traditional spiritual umbilical cord holding soul to body. I can believe and be reassured by these accounts, but it was not my own experience. The restlessness, the agony of each breath was not what I was prepared for. A friend said exactly the same thing to me recently, after being with her dying sister. Geoff Hall had already warned me: 'Dying can be a very unpleasant experience.' But, incurable romantic that I am, I had clung on to a different vision.

Some people think of death as the birth of the soul; if so, I witnessed a difficult birth.

I wrote this poem on a beautiful September morning, the autumn before Charlie died. It is not one that I could have shown him.

Winter

Draped in expensive silk of feather grey
the valley wears September like a shawl;
a scarf of birdsong flaunts about its neck
jet beads of blackberries glitter round its throat
– but oh my Love of many summer days
how frayed and wintery now your wind-thin coat!

The ever fashion-conscious countryside
which always keeps its wardrobe up to date
knows it will sport a bright new dress each May,
but time's run out for me to hope and cling
or try to patch again the wearied cloth
that will not last you for another spring.

Can I be strong enough to wave goodbye
dressed in the laugh you've always loved so much
and try to keep my tears for underclothes?
I wish that I could unstitch all the pain
that you have worn so long with such panache
and make your sad rags whole and new again.

Cradle-song

This year
we had a cradle
at the foot of our bed.

Oh not the kind we used to have
where slumbering babies slept
securely wrapped,
but one that kept the bed-clothes
off your legs:
even the lightest sheet
put too much pressure
on your shell-thin feet.

Now you are gone
covers lie flat again
but the weight of your absence
is a blanket of heaviness.

I knew we had to part
and do rejoice
at your relief from pain,
but how I long to hear your voice
– that vibrant baritone
which often reached
further than you intended, for
you had no whisper.

I wish I had a cradle
to keep this grief
from pressing on my heart.

Part Four

We took comfort from planning Charlie's funeral service. He'd always had a strong Christian faith and, not an ex-headmaster for nothing (our children used to say, 'Give Dad three people and he's got a class'), he had liked arranging services himself, so we knew what his loves and hates were. Successive vicars of Arthington, of which Charlie was patron, had sometimes been terrorized or infuriated (or both) by his tendency to take over, but our present vicar, Denys de la Hoyde, was different. Though he had only known Charlie in the years since his stroke, they respected each other and got on extremely well. Denys was not only amused by Charlie – and he could stand up to him – he also loved him.

Ceremonies are important rites of passage that help us to accept change. We were determined to give Charlie a wonderful send-off and make his service as personal and memorable as possible. Our problem lay not in wondering what to have, but in deciding what to leave out, both in music and in words. In the end I think we were all happy that our choice combined Charlie's own favourites with things which were of special comfort to us. Because there would be a memorial service at the school in the summer, we knew we would have a second chance to include other things later.

Sometimes decisions about funeral services have to be taken in a rush, but we had over a week. Charlie died on a

Monday, but the following weekend was the wedding of one of Susannah's closest friends, and we were anxious not to cast any cloud over that joyful occasion, at which Sue's daughter, Hermione, was to be a bridesmaid. On that Saturday, Sue and Robert, with Hermione looking as pretty as a flower fairy, went off to the wedding and left me with the two boys: Freddie, the baby, and young William, aged six and a half.

I shall never forget the conversation I had with him that day. All the older children had been very sad at the news, but William, not a little boy to wear his heart on his sleeve, had been particularly upset, and cried and cried. Since then he had refused to talk about it, and Susannah was worried about him.

We had a happy afternoon, took the dogs out for a walk and bumped Freddie in his pram along the path through the woods. Then we came in for tea and lit the fire. William plonked himself down in the chair that Charlie had always sat in.

'Granny,' he said. 'Do you ever want to talk about Grandpa, or do you *never* want to talk about him?'

'Well,' I said cautiously, knowing this might be important, and anxious not to get it wrong. 'There are times when I need to talk about him very much, when it helps me. But I suppose there are other times when I feel I can't, either because it hurts too much, or because it feels private at that particular moment. On the whole, I want to talk.'

He sat and digested this in silence, then he gave me a brilliant smile. 'I see,' he said. 'I see. So, it's really all right to do what you feel like?'

'Yes,' I said.

'Let's talk about him then,' he said. So we did. I think

it is interesting that this little boy voiced so clearly what often remains a problem for much older people. So often people find it hard to broach the subject of death to the bereaved. Perhaps our airing of the subject that day will stand this child in good stead later in life, and help him to feel at ease with making approaches to friends who have suffered a loss.

During the rest of that summer, he would often bring up the subject of his grandfather when he came to stay. 'It's a nice feeling,' he said to me one day when the children were helping me water pot plants in the greenhouse, 'to think we're looking after Grandpa's flowers for him.'

Three years later I drew on this conversation for my second novel, putting the words in the mouth of an older child and in very different circumstances. Children are as baffled as we are about how to deal with grief. Because they may not always be able to speak about it – as this reserved, but articulate, child could – it does not mean they don't feel it deeply.

Belinda, Susannah and I, with the help of kind neighbours, went mad with flowers both for the church and in the house. It looked more as if a wedding were about to take place.

On the morning of the funeral three things happened almost simultaneously. Brian Johnston, Charlie's lifelong friend, together with his wife, Pauline, arrived from London for lunch. 'Now we shall have a breath of fresh air to cheer us up,' said Belinda as we greeted this magically funny man, to whom we were all devoted. But Brian walked into the house with tears pouring down his face and could hardly speak. The van from the florist's arrived with all the family's floral tributes – and also another van, with a flashing light, out of which burst four burly security men. One of the grandchildren had mistaken my mobile panic-button for the remote-control switch of the television, and set off the burglar alarm.

'I suppose they're looking for the body,' said someone. It seemed extraordinarily funny, and we became hysterical with unsuitable mirth. The line between laughter and tears can be a very fine one – but the release of emotion is good either way.

The church, which easily seats three hundred people, was packed. I felt intensely proud of my children. William read the lesson from St John, 'In the beginning was the Word', which we had so often heard Charlie read at Christmas. We all knew how emotional Will felt, but he had indignantly turned down the offer to have someone standing by in case he was overcome at the last moment. 'I shall manage,' he said fiercely – and he did, clearly and beautifully. I have heard him read lessons before and since, but never quite like he read that day. Many people commented on it afterwards. On the other hand, Brian Johnston, that veteran broadcaster, reading the wonderful passage on death by Canon Henry Scott-Holland, nearly came unstuck – and that was deeply moving too. We have a brilliant organist at Arthington, and he did us proud. Apart from favourites such as 'Nimrod' from Elgar's *Enigma Variations*, and some much-loved Bach and Handel, those who could recognize it noted the tribute to Charlie's love of opera in selections from Wagner and Verdi. Listening to music from *La Traviata* nearly undid one friend. Denys gave a wonderful address, which was both touching and funny. It was a tribute to the courage and humour of an unusual man – but no whitewash job either, something Charlie, the least pretentious of men and a loather of humbug, would have hated. Lots of people wrote to me afterwards asking for copies of the address. We sang Charlie's favourite hymns.

Recently I have been to two funerals where the committal has taken place immediately before the service in church, and have thought what a good way round this is. It allows the close family privacy at the grave, and gets the worst part of the funeral over first. The sight of the coffin disappearing, either into the earth or through curtains at a crematorium, is a very desolate one, though possibly important in stressing the total finality of death. We did not think of doing things this way round at the time, but perhaps it is worth mentioning as a possible alternative.

The following morning, I went over to the churchyard to look at the flowers and read the cards on them. The stonemason employed by the undertaker was already there, starting to replace the wall and railings round the entrance to the family vault. Rather to my surprise, he asked me about Charlie's education, which he had read about in an obituary. It turned out that his son was a master at Eton, and had just been told that he was soon to become a housemaster. We sat together on the grass in the April sunshine, and I told him about Charlie's schooldays and of my own childhood there, and he told me of his pride in this brilliant son of his, who had got a classical scholarship to university. Charlie would have loved this conversation.

I think it might be worth mentioning here an incident which brought me great comfort. It may not be acceptable to everyone, but in case anyone else finds it comforting I feel I should record it. Make of it what you will.

I have already mentioned that I belonged to a doctors' and healers' network, of which our own doctor was also a member. At that time, the quarterly meetings were held in either his surgery or our house. One of the healers, Wendy, had met Charlie, who liked her enormously and appreciated her sense of humour and straightforward attitudes. She did not know him well and had only met him as an elderly invalid, sitting in his chair in a dressing-gown.

Wendy and several other healers used to go once a week to give healing at Cookridge Hospital in Leeds in the oncology unit. The week Charlie died, Wendy had a 'visit' from Charlie that woke her up at three o'clock in the morning. Some people might prefer to call this a vision. She had not known he'd died, and was worried about what my reaction would be if she rang me up. It was her day for the hospital, and she asked two of her fellow healers what she should do. They had seen the announcement of Charlie's death in the paper and suggested she should get in touch with me. I received a letter from Wendy saying she had something to tell me, but only if I felt like hearing it, and would leave it to me to get in touch if I wanted to. Of course I rang her up.

This is the story. Charlie came and stood at the foot of Wendy's bed and said he had a message for me. 'Tell Mary I'm all right,' he said. She said she recognized him, but that he looked very different – younger, taller and much darker. Charlie had lost several inches in height over the last years, and when I married him he had had very dark hair. Then she became hesitant. 'What I'm going to tell you now may be offensive to you,' she said cautiously. I told her to go ahead. She said he had been wearing 'rather an odd suit' but that it seemed terribly important. He kept pointing at it as if it was highly significant. I asked her to describe it. 'Well,' she said nervously. 'It was rather flash – sort of dandified. Not what I would have expected him to wear at all. It was double-breasted and had wide lapels.' She went on to describe the material in detail: a grey flannel with distinctive chalk stripes – white and red. My hair stood on end.

I knew that suit, though I certainly hadn't given it a thought for well over thirty years. It was Charlie's demob suit – the free issue which everyone in the forces received after the war. When we were first married I thought it perfectly ghastly and made at least two fruitless attempts to give it to a jumble sale. Charlie rescued it and insisted on wearing it when he umpired cricket matches, as a tease, though he didn't really like it himself. It became a private joke between us. It took me about a year to banish it for good, but it had gone well before Belinda was born. No one but me could have possibly known about it.

Of course I told my children. They were as enchanted as I was – it was such a very typical Charlie story. To all of us, it had the ring of truth. 'But if Dad could manage to get in touch, why couldn't he have appeared to you himself?' William asked. 'Because Wendy had a telephone and I didn't,' I said. I am still quite happy with this explanation, and I made notes of my conversation with Wendy at the time of the event. It helped to ease the ache of missing him, the knowledge that I would never speak to him again.

There is a sense of anticlimax once a funeral is over. So many people say they have got through the first week after a death, either in a semi-anaesthetized state – on automatic pilot as it were – or buoyed up on the extra adrenalin our bodies produce in a crisis, which can make the bereaved feel curiously 'high'. This can be very disconcerting.

After that, the long process of facing the daunting void and adapting to change begins – and there is no extra boost to see one through that. What there is, though, is an extraordinary amount of kindness, sometimes from unexpected people, and this awareness of love and of imaginative thoughtfulness is like a series of lanterns on a dark path. People left little offerings on the doorstep: books they had found helpful themselves, pot plants or something cooked to put in the deep freeze. All the postmen on our round sent me a card, with a tribute to Charlie, signed by all five of them. Friends rang up to check on me. All these things warmed my cold cockles – and made me regret that I had not always been so imaginative for other people myself. I longed to talk about Charlie, and it was helpful when people made this easy.

One thing that bothered me was that, as the widow, I was very much put in the starring role, and I wondered if my children, so generous in their support for me, received enough support themselves. I had lost the companion of the best part of my life, but they had lost a very beloved father. In fact, they have all told me since that sharing my grief helped them too, and that they were especially thankful not to be shut out from Charlie's final illness and death. I have got so much wrong, but it's a comfort to know that perhaps I got this bit more or less right. In an effort to spare others pain – or to prevent them from witnessing our own – it is all too easy to exclude people, and not let them make their own farewells to a dying or dead person and express their own sadness.

I received over five hundred letters about Charlie. They were not just from close friends or old pupils: they came from some unexpected quarters and from all walks of life. Death gives people a chance to say things they might never otherwise put into words. I found the letters a great comfort, and still do. I think I answered them all in the end, though I had a gap when I 'dried up' and stopped for a couple of months. I don't think anyone, especially not anyone who has gone through a bereavement themselves, expects a quick response, or even any response. If you set yourself too high a standard about the speed of answering letters, then what should be a comfort becomes one more pressure. A stock of postcards can be useful. Some people have cards printed with a message. Some people don't do anything, and that's all right too.

I remember going into Harrogate the week after the funeral and automatically checking my watch in a panic. I realized that, for the first time in years, it didn't matter how long I was away. The freedom from anxiety was extraordinary. I had no idea how much a part of me that constant worry had become. It felt very strange.

A few months before Charlie died, there had been pressure for me to take another break – a proper holiday this time. The Australian nurse who had helped me out before was once again over here, and Belinda and I had planned to go to Majorca for a week in May. We had taken out insurance against unexpected cancellation, and over the last month I had wanted to cancel. I knew I could not have left Charlie at this stage. However, our doctor had begged me not to call it off yet. He was proved right: three weeks after Charlie's death Belinda and I flew off for what was to be a wonderfully happy week.

I am not saying there were not moments when we both felt very sad – of course there were – but the feeling of living on a smoking volcano had gone, and the long haul of coping with loneliness and facing difficult decisions had not really set in. Like the Hellenic cruise all those years before, it was an oasis. When I look back on that week I do not only think of mourning: I remember ripe oranges and the smell of orange blossom; blue sea and sky; walking through the olive groves round Deia and finding wild cyclamen on the hills; some tears, much laughter; but above all, freedom from worry and the torment of watching someone else's pain.

We invented the life histories of our fellow guests in the hotel, and gave them all imaginary names. There was Victor, the understanding gynaecologist, adored by his doting women patients – but not by his grumpy wife, Muriel – as he twinkled understandingly at them over his hospital mask. Actually, he probably sold second-hand cars, or massaged accounts, and she may have been as cosy as furry bedroom slippers. There was the glitzy German pair who looked straight out of *Dynasty* or *Dallas*, and the fatherly small-town solicitor with his socially ambitious wife. Our imaginations ran riot. No doubt they would all have been most surprised had they known about their *alter egos*. In the unlikely event that any of them were playing the same game, I don't think they would have cast us as a bereaved mother and daughter. 'Thank God I wasn't there to hear you two shrieking with laughter,' said my son-in-law Charles, whose generous suggestion it had been to spare Belinda to come with me.

We swam and read books, we ate and lay in the sun. And we talked and talked: about the past and the future; about Belinda's children and her anxieties about her handicapped son, James; about my hopes and fears for Arthington and the rebuilding of my life.

It was a precious week, and strengthened me for all the uncertainties to come. I did not at all want to go home, and remember feeling utterly panic-stricken on the last evening at the thought of the problems that lay ahead.

One thing I had already faced was sleeping alone in the house. For the first week I'd had the family with me. After the funeral they were anxious that I should accept the offers of kind friends to come and spend nights at Arthington, but I wanted to confront the emptiness as soon as possible. Though it is a very big house, and down a long drive – not what some people would consider cosy – it was my home and I adored it. Also it was summer, which makes a big difference, and I had three dogs for company.

This business of getting used to living alone – and I am not talking about loneliness here so much as nervousness – is very individual. Some people need to adjust gradually. I think the secret is not to do it for too long at a time – little and often is what helped me most. The family were very good and tried to take it in turns to come up most weekends to start with. It is important to have things planned which you can look forward to, with bite-sized intervals between them. I have learnt that for me it is foolish to allow myself to look at frightening films on television or read scary books. The creaking board or the wuthering wind, which I can ignore when there is someone else near, can seem threatening in isolation, especially if you have a vivid imagination.

Loneliness, which can bite just as hard amongst a crowd as in solitude, is another matter. A friend of ours who had lost his beloved wife about six months earlier, gave me a piece of advice. 'The trick is,' he said, 'to organize your life so that you are alone as little as possible. Ask people in, or arrange to go out. I try to have as few evenings on my own as possible.' For him this has been a brilliant coping strategy and I admire, and perhaps envy, the way he manages to entertain so often and so well, and lead a busy social life; but even as he said this, I knew it was not the right way for me. I felt I needed to face my loneliness from the start, to stare at the wall if need be, and get used to the empty space in my heart. Otherwise I was afraid I might always be on the run from it.

We are all different in our needs. There is no right way to come to terms with bereavement, though I do think it is important to have someone to whom one can talk. Talking can be a lifeline when moments of desperation strike, and the helplines which so many organizations now have seem to me a brilliant idea.

The clearing out of someone's belongings after death is a painful process. Again there is no right way, or right time. Too precipitate action can later bring regrets, and can seem like a denial of the person who has gone. If it is left too long it may get harder and harder to do. In the case of a child, I think it must be supremely difficult.

With older relations, parents for instance, there can also be a terrible feeling of prying and intrusion, of suddenly becoming privy to information to which one is not entitled. There may be little relics and reminders of one's own childhood. There may be many things which one is tempted to keep but simply has not room to store. There are many hard decisions.

In Charlie's case, I tackled his clothes and personal possessions very quickly. If he had died suddenly in his prime, I am sure I wouldn't have been able to do this so soon and might have felt I was betraying him, but I had found it hard that our bedroom had turned so completely into a sick-room over the last few years, and I hated all the medical equipment that filled it – the cradle to hold the bedclothes up, the sheepskin for him to lie on, the paraphernalia for coping with incontinence, all the pills. These couldn't vanish fast enough. It had always been difficult to get Charlie to part with old clothes or buy new ones – witness Wendy's story of the suit

– and some of his things were now not only shabby beyond belief, but to me had the aura of illness about them. These I could not wait to part with, though disposing of his long-unworn skiing clothes cost me an awful pang.

I had in Mary Pennington, daughter of Pen my old decorating guru, the perfect person to help me start on the preliminary throwing-away session. Mary is a dear friend who has worked for and with me for over thirty years, though how she has stuck my general scattiness I'll never know. She is not only unfailingly supportive and loving, but practical and unsentimental. She is also brilliant at all the things at which I am worst, so perhaps we make a good team.

We sorted clothes into three categories: burn, send to St George's Crypt in Leeds, and consult the family. We filled endless black bin liners, and Mary firmly prevented me from leaving the job half finished – a failing of mine of which she rightly disapproves. I am a procrastination junkie.

Some of his good clothes were convertible for use by my son and sons-in-law. It gave me joy, and would have pleased Charlie, that William wore to his own wedding the morning coat that had been made for Charlie for ours. William is taller than Charlie, but the cut was perfect. Perhaps the psychedelic brilliance of William's silk waistcoat might have been looked on askance in 1953 – I think his father-in-law was rather startled by it in 1991 – but I'm sure Charlie, with his penchant for bright colours, would have approved of that too.

There was one garment I couldn't part with and kept for myself. This was a very soft and light quilted Puffa jacket, which I had bought for Charlie about two years before he died, when his customary old tweed jackets became too heavy for his fragile frame to support. He had loved it. After he died I wore it constantly, and felt some sense of closeness to him by doing so. One day, fishing in the pocket for a hanky, I found an old glove – just one left-hand one. I looked in a cupboard in the gun-room at Arthington, a treasure trove of odd socks, gloves and old hats, to see if I could find its pair, but it wasn't there. I remember thinking the glove was like me: I too was without my partner now. I sat on the floor surrounded by old gloves feeling obsolete and desolate, wondering how I was going to find a new sense of purpose, without leaning too heavily on my ever-tolerant and loving children and grandchildren. It is one thing to be a helpful granny: it is another to lead one's life at second-hand.

Such apparently trivial things can trigger off a bout of grieving. As it happened, this incident triggered off a poem too, which I have included at the end of this section.

A year later, returning from a week on the island of Iona, I threw the Puffa, along with other clothes, into the washing machine. I was greeted next morning by clouds of steam billowing down the passage. The thermostat on my old machine had given up the ghost and the clothes had been boiling merrily all night. The water was a rich witch's brew of purple, but the Puffa was a limp and shrunken rag of indeterminate colour. I minded very much at the time; it seemed one more severed link, but perhaps it was a good thing really: it had served its purpose.

I had a new difficulty now. We all agreed that my mother could not be left in her self-contained flat if I was away, but everyone also agreed that after such a long period of being completely tied to Charlie, I should not exchange one tether for another. Up to now her need had combined with his.

Anyone who saw that enchanting American film *Driving*

Miss Daisy will have seen much of my mother's character. Everything that was most admirable, infuriating, lovable and difficult about Miss Daisy, was my mother to a tee. Help was available if she chose to use it, but like Miss Daisy she could be resistant. When she and my father first came to live at Arthington, we leased them the lodge at the end of the drive so that they could have someone working for them, independently of us. My mother often gave her helpers a rough ride, but they usually adored her. To outside observers it may have looked obvious that she should now move into the main house with me – but I don't think anyone who knew either of us well would have considered this a workable option for a moment. We found a compromise in the form of a special alarm bell, supposedly always to be worn as a pendant round the neck. If activated, it rang through to a main switchboard who would call first my number, then her doctor's, then the police. She pressed it with great regularity to check it was working properly and to keep us on our toes, but seldom actually wore it.

The routine advice, that you should wait a year after the death of a partner before making any major change, is wise, though not always possible. I was to undergo many changes of heart and mind, and swung giddily between optimism and despair.

I had known there would be big changes to be faced, and that ill-health had caused Charlie to let our affairs slip dangerously out of control for a long time. Indeed I had sometimes connived at this, begging our advisers not to put pressure on him, because I knew what a bad effect anxiety had on his health. I had not realized quite how bad things were. I had guessed we would have to alter our lifestyle and try to turn the property to some commercial use, but had never seriously considered parting with it. I was convinced someone – probably me, I modestly thought – would come up with a bright idea. I came up with ideas all right. They just weren't viable. There were debts to be paid.

To say the shoe was beginning to pinch would be an unsuitable metaphor: it was more like a very small foot sliding hopelessly round in a porous, gigantic old boot, with no socks for padding.

My brother and our solicitor were trustees, and with my interests at heart, they had the unenviable task of trying to make me look at realities – building a little house in one of the walled gardens, or looking for one somewhere else – but, above all, facing up to selling Arthington. The prospect of this seemed a bereavement too many, another knife in my heart from which, so soon after Charlie's death, I felt I might haemorrhage. I'd also hoped to be able to hand it on to our son. They tried gently to make me see sense. I can *see* sense as well as anyone – it's just that I'm not usually much drawn to it.

I would hate to give the impression that there was anything specially difficult or unusual in my circumstances. There wasn't. Many widows, perhaps most, have to face a move for a variety of reasons, and the place in which one's children have grown up and where one has been especially happy, always represents a nest which it is hard to leave. If the house in question has been in the family for many generations perhaps it seems hard to be the one who breaks a chain, but I knew I'd been lucky to live there at all. I had huge financial worries, but I also had assets beyond some people's dreams.

One of the things that had been difficult during Charlie's

illness was that I had increasingly had to take the reins of our marriage into my own hands, while trying to pretend that this was not so. I found it hard to be forced into the driving seat and yet try to disguise the fact that I was the one who was driving – it must have been even harder for Charlie to be forced out of the driving seat by ill-health. Now I still had to drive – but with no passenger, no one else to consult a map with me or share the journey. I found this very difficult. Sometimes I still do. It felt as if my steering was all over the road.

That first summer was an extremely busy one. In June, William and Alice became engaged, and this was a bright light in our landscape. In early July we had a memorial service for Charlie in the school chapel. The Dawsons, who had taken over from Charlie, were kindness itself – nothing was too much trouble – and Sarah Wood, who taught music, was determined that the choir should not only learn all the things we wanted but should excel themselves – which they did.

Driving south for the service, to stay with Belinda and Charles in Wandsworth, I got lost. I couldn't believe it. I had driven from Arthington to London countless times and knew the route extremely well. At the end of the MI I usually took a short cut via Cricklewood to South Kensington to miss the traffic round Marble Arch. I must have missed a turning in Cricklewood, but to this day I don't really know what I did. I suddenly realized that I hadn't the faintest idea where I was, and no signpost said anything familiar. In the rush hour it wasn't possible to stop. I ended up south of Hampton Court. At least that gave me my bearings again. I was shaking with fright and exhaustion by the time I eventually arrived and Belinda and Charles had started to worry.

When we are bereaved, we think we are acting normally and are totally in charge, and it can be extremely scary to find this is not so.

I had expected to enjoy the thanksgiving service. We had planned to make it as joyful as possible, and all agreed to wear our brightest clothes in Charlie's honour. What I had not taken into account was the flood of memories of our early married years which hit me like a tidal wave. The Dawsons gave a wonderful tea party in the garden after the service. It seemed weird to be standing in the sunshine chatting to friends, many of whom were ex-pupils or parents, as I had so often done in the past at Sports Days. It was like a rerun of an old film – except that the main star, the one vital person, was missing. Lots of people told me it was wonderful to see me in such sparkling form. Actually I thought I was going to die.

While writing this chapter I discussed with one of my daughters this strange difference between other people's perceptions of how we are, and what we actually feel like inside. She told me for the first time how worried those closest to me had been about my behaviour during the week of Charlie's funeral. I had thought I was particularly calm and in control, taking good decisions, and in charge of myself and everything else. Apparently they thought I talked rubbish half the time, was fixated about small, unimportant details, irrational and almost overexcited. I was sublimely unaware of this. I am glad she has told me now, because I think it is relevant to pass this on – but I'm also relieved to discover she no longer thinks it's a problem!

The evening of Charlie's memorial service, Bamber Gascoigne, who had read a lesson at the service, had invited me to go with him and Christina to a performance of *Tosca* at Covent Garden with Placido Domingo and Maria Ewing. It was a fantastic invitation, but after we got back to London, I knew I couldn't make it. I was utterly finished. Opera had been a specially shared pleasure between Charlie and me, and I hadn't yet been to one without him. It had been crazy of me to think I would be able to manage it. I asked Belinda to go in my stead.

I am so glad she refused to do this and made me go. It was a wonderful evening and proved to be a catharsis. When I went to bed that night I felt I had experienced every emotion in the book.

There are many difficulties over one's own behaviour to be coped with in the early days after a bereavement. Soon after Charlie's death, in a determined effort not to let my newly bereaved state cast a pall over a weekend for a special occasion, I was taken aback to find my sparkling display of false tinsel had apparently been mistaken for a flashing green light by a married man. I refused an innocuous ensuing invitation. Though I was genuinely unable to accept, what utterly amazed me was that this perfectly ordinary refusal was greeted with so much surprise – and anger. I was mortified to discover afterwards that my acceptance had been the subject of a bet. When you have become used to living within the confines and security of a long and close marriage, it takes time to adjust to the discovery that these have been removed. After a bereavement all emotions are exaggerated and small pinpricks seem magnified: this trivial incident put me back a long way with my struggle to feel socially assured again. I have since heard many other widows complain of the same sort of thing. It must be much more difficult for younger women – or, I suppose, men.

On the other side of the coin, it has to be said that there is only a fine line between generous help towards someone who is vulnerable and over-involvement. Widows can seem threatening to wives.

It is impossible to know how one is going to react to all sorts of occasions: it can be disconcerting when activities or situations that have previously been a delight can either be a torment, or leave one unexpectedly cold. We try to rekindle old fires and find the wood is damp. Or the flames of enjoyment start to burn, only to be suddenly doused when exhaustion hits us like a bucket of water. After a major blow, sometimes ordinary things can seem trivial and make us impatient or judgemental of other people. There are many adjustments to be made, and I found it difficult to adjust to my new freedom.

Two weeks after Charlie's death, Jim, our one remaining garden help, had a minor stroke. Happily he recovered, but obviously he had to retire. I had never been a hands-on gardener, but that summer the garden obsessed me. I kept thinking a reproachful figure might zoom round a corner in an electric buggy and be distressed by the total disintegration of something he had made so beautiful.

Various gardening pals of Charlie's generously gave occasional help, but the whole thing was galloping out of control; really this had started long before he died. I had no idea the wilderness could encroach so fast. In the past we had sold soft fruit and tomatoes. By July it was hardly possible to struggle into the fruit cage for brambles and nettles, and the famous herbaceous border was a jungle.

I tried to thin the grapes in the vinery and went out to the peach house very early every morning and late each night to spray against red-spider – that dreaded invisible wrecker of hothouse fruit, for whose invasion head gardeners could be sacked in the past. I was determined that when the family all came to stay in August the bumper crops would be perfect for them. It was a terrible waste of energy: in the event, just before the fruit was ripe, grey squirrels got through one of the many holes in the broken glass that I had failed to net, and stripped the trees completely. To add insult to injury half the fruit just lay on the ground, ruined but not completely demolished. I felt utter despair.

I decided that, whether I could afford it or not, I must have help in the garden, and so I advertised. At this stage I still had no idea what I was going to do, but had not yet given up hope of a salvage operation. To let the garden go completely seemed the ultimate betrayal of Charlie – far worse than disposing of his clothes. A marvellous girl answered my advertisement. She had been the top student at her horticultural college and I could have read her references in the dark: they glowed. I couldn't pay her half what she could have earned elsewhere, but the more I showed her the horrors of decay, the more she wanted to help me reclaim the garden. My dottiness must have been catching.

She lived ten miles away, was not on the telephone and could not drive a car; I had no vacant cottage to offer her, and there was no transport in our village. Undaunted, we made a plan. We would leave a bicycle in the shed of a kind farmer in the next village on a bus route. She would get there on the bus and then bicycle the three miles to Arthington. If the weather was terrible and I was at home, I would meet her in the car and we would cram the bike in the back. If I was away and she decided to turn tail and go home on the bus, or if it was sufficiently foul for her not to come, then that was all right by me. I can't think of anyone else who would have contemplated such a job.

She set about trying to reclaim the garden with enormous energy and method, but it was a labour of Hercules. This arrangement lasted, unbelievably, for six months until the following February. I can't think how she stuck it so long. Then the appalling weather, the broken glass, collapsing outbuildings and the impossibility of it all overcame us both. I felt I could not possibly stand in the way of her career and she accepted a job with Leeds City Parks. She tried to work a miracle while she was with me and I shall always be grateful. We both cried when she left, and we are still in touch.

I realize that these experiences may not seem relevant. Not many widows have such huge and crumbly dwellings; perhaps not many are so foolish as to whack their heads so stubbornly against brick walls, but perhaps it illustrates how hard it is to face a major change at a time of bereavement, and how much one's judgement can be impaired. I have heard of people who have taken the opposite road to me, and made the most sensible and practical-seeming decisions too soon – and regretted those later too. The details don't really matter: it is trial, error and perseverance before we eventually find a new vision, and accept change. Old habits die hard: if widowhood coincides with a time when all the chicks have flown the nest it is necessary to reassess one's role. This can bring a new sense of freedom, but it takes time and courage to seize new opportunities and make a new existence, to realize that we are no longer a key player in the drama of family life.

Of course, some people make provision for their future before the death of a spouse. Perhaps it was bad luck that

Charlie's strategy of refusing to admit defeat, which also made him so brave and indomitable, such a survivor, made it impossible for me to discuss the future with him much earlier on, but I have absolutely no regrets about this. You do the best you can with a given situation – you can't always expect to get it right.

Recollections of those first months after Charlie's death have fused together. I can't always remember what I did or felt at particular times. Looking back, there seems to have been a surprising amount of fun, spiked with moments of intense desolation and sadness.

After Charlie had become reclusive, I led a very re-stricted life, and sometimes felt extremely isolated. Had it not been for the imaginative generosity of some close friends I might have been completely out of practice for any social life. Over the early years of Charlie's illness, they had gone on inviting us to do things long after we felt we had to refuse other invitations: they always said, 'Don't worry if you can't make it.' When outings became impossible for him, they continued to ask me to go to concerts, or do things with them – but always with the same understanding that I might have to let them down at the last minute. Because they lived so near, this was occasionally possible, when I would never have gone further afield. It was a lifeline.

When we first went to live at Arthington, a new acquaint-ance asked me if I could help her out with a 'widows' lunch'. I assumed that she meant some charity function, but she explained that it was just a way of clearing her social decks of 'all those single women'. So difficult to find spare men, she said, and it saved one from having uneven numbers. Even in the sixties, when country dinner parties tended to be more formal than they are now, I remember being horrified at this ghetto approach, and thinking how awful it would be to be deprived of mixed society just because one had no partner. I am happy to say that my own experience has been very different. After her husband died, a friend of mine told me how much she appreciated married neighbours who used to invite her to walk her dogs with them and always took care to see that she walked in the middle. Only the other day, when I arrived at the church for a wedding, I was touched when a couple I don't know very well invited me to go and sit with them and insisted that I sat between them. These small imaginative sensitivities can mean a great deal.

All sorts of friends now started to ask me to do things I'd been unable to do for years. The kindness I received was amazing. Of course, I had to get used to doing things alone. I think many bereaved people would agree that it is not so much the going out alone – though this can take courage – but the coming home alone that is the worst bit. There is no one to share amusement or enjoyment with – no one to 'tell it to'. I still miss this very much.

At the end of November, Will and Alice got married. I could not have been more delighted at the prospect of Alice as a daughter-in-law. I loved her from the start and she has become the dearest friend.

Alice's parents gave our young couple a wonderful wedding, and I was thankful I could attend without the torment of leaving a very sick Charlie behind. All the same, without him at my side for this very special occasion, the prospect was something of an ordeal: the exhaustion that comes with a major bereavement could still totally overwhelm me without warning, leaving me feeling as if my life force was seeping into the ground; I still felt emotionally unreliable and was terrified I might break down and cry – which would not have mattered normally, but was the last thing I wanted to be seen to do on such a joyful occasion. As it turned out, I was genuinely able to enjoy it, though it had its poignant moments. I felt very proud of our son and wished his father could have seen him.

It was a relief that I managed to get my mother there. She had initially said she was too old to make the journey to Scotland in the winter, but none of us took this seriously. She loved it all and was on cracking form.

In mid-December, when Will and Alice got back from their honeymoon, I gave a party for them at Arthington. The complete lack of confidence for entertaining which was to hit me later – and from which to some extent I still suffer – had clearly not set in. Arthington is a wonderful house for parties and looked its beguiling best. I felt more than ever determined to try to hang on to it. Looking back on that first year of bereavement, I can see that what I was really trying to do was not to look to the future and make a new life, but to re-create a bit of the past which I had once specially enjoyed but which had gone for good.

A large number of my family live in Scotland, but I was not so lucky in getting my mother there a second time that winter. We none of us wanted to Christmas at Arthington, the scene of so many wonderful family gatherings in the past, and Belinda and Charles had asked me to go to them. This meant that Will and Alice could Christmas with her parents, I would be able to see them too, and could drop my mother off with my brother *en route*. My car was already loaded up with Christmas presents on the night before we were to drive north together, when my mother had a heart attack. There was no way she could travel, and no way that I could desert her.

She hated being the cause of this change of plan and I felt terribly sorry for her, but all the same I battled with myself over inner resentment. I knew it was unfair of me. I really don't think I let her see – but I had a nasty, demoralizing little attack of self-pity. In the end, the one thing everyone had been determined to avoid, happened: I had Christmas alone at Arthington.

Festivals, like anniversaries, force memories on us. I had found it incredibly difficult to attend the carol service at Arthington church a week before – actually I still find that hard after four years. In some ways this disaster was an odd sort of blessing. I remember sitting alone on Christmas night, feeling utterly bleak, but also really forcing myself to face the future. Despite anxious and loving calls from all the family, emotionally I hit rock bottom that weekend. When you have hit the bottom there is nowhere to go but up.

Luckily my mother made a wonderful recovery.

It took a trip to India to enable me to let go of my dream of keeping Arthington and to face forwards.

In February I went with Robin and Lilias Sheepshanks on a package tour of Rajasthan. Holidays can be a problem when you are on your own, and it was wonderful to go with them: I knew them so well that no social effort was required, and they never made me feel that two was company and I just a spare third.

I had always longed to go to India, but was half afraid to see the Taj Mahal in case its famous magic should escape me, and I should feel myself excluded – like failing a test, or not being selected for a team at some dreaded children's party. I need not have worried. None of the clichés had prepared me for its impact. We were lucky enough to watch it turn pink at sunset and then float like a water lily on the mist at dawn early next morning. I half expected to see the hand of God suddenly stretch down and remove it before my eyes, like an ivory chess piece.

People say you cannot go to India and come back unchanged. It was certainly so for me. It is hard to explain. It has something to do with India's vastness and extremes: the poverty is so terrible, the riches so wonderful; its history is so immense; there are so many contrasts, so much that is inexplicable to western ways of thought; above all, there are the teeming millions of people. Perhaps, too, something about their different attitude to life and death is almost in the air you breathe.

After the conducted tour was over, Robin, Lilias and I went a little further south and stayed on for a few extra days in a vast maharajah's palace, now partly a hotel, but still lived in by the original family. It had a sinister sense of bloodthirsty history. Unfortunately, the only rooms available happened to be suites: it was probably fun for two – a bit of a lark – but I rattled about in mine like shaking bones. It may sound the acme of luxury, but nothing could be guaranteed to underline new aloneness more than a vast and gloomy set of rooms all to oneself. I was also absolutely terrified there. As the huge, brass-studded wooden door clanged shut behind me at night, setting up echoes and leaving me to face the shadowy corners of my unsuitable accommodation, the hair rose up on the back of my neck. Perhaps it also forced me to look at some shadowy corners in myself.

I did not take a conscious decision about any particular course of action while I was there, but on one sleepless night, I went out by myself into the courtyard and sat listening to the unfamiliar sounds of an Indian night and gazing up at the stars. As I sat there alone, I was suddenly overwhelmed by a feeling of my own insignificant smallness in the whole pattern of things. I wondered why I was making such heavy weather about letting go of possessions and a particular way of life instead of just getting on with living – with gratitude.

It was the oppressiveness of my quarters that sent me out into the Indian darkness on that particular night, but it had a profound effect on me and gave me a much-needed shift of consciousness. Perhaps if this had not happened I should not now be living in my present house or writing this book.

The weekend after I got back from India, I looked at the property section of the newspaper. There was a cottage advertised in a village above the Washburn valley. I made an appointment to look at it and asked a friend to come with me, just for fun. The cottage was up a hill on a twisty country lane. It was charming, well set back from the road, and very old. Everything was in immaculate condition and it had a perfectly manicured garden. It would be many people's idea of a dream cottage, but I have always been very affected by light, and knew that the low beamed ceilings and small windows would oppress me. I made polite noises, but said it was not what I wanted. The agent said that by chance, another cottage nearby had just been put on the market too. Perhaps I would like to see that while I was here. I wasn't keen, already regretting the impulse that had sent me house hunting, but it seemed silly not to look.

The moment I stood on the doorstep, before I had even seen inside, I knew I was going to live there. It really was as simple as that. I felt the house had found me. I had made a list of my basic requirements – it had none of them. What it had was a great feeling of light and tranquillity, and a lovely view.

I was amazed by the enthusiastic response of my family. It made me realize just how gently they had been trying to treat me. They all came to look, and were as convinced as I was that it would be exactly right.

I felt extraordinarily strengthened that I had made this – to me – momentous decision. That is not to say that I did not find the prospect of parting with beloved Arthington utterly heart-rending. We all did. But I felt I had taken a positive step into the future and done something on my own initiative.

I could not then know that events were going to change unexpectedly after I left Arthington. My son, William, was moved up to Yorkshire by his firm, and he and his family are now living there. The house was on the market for over a year but it did not sell – apparently not everyone sees the charm of large derelict rooms and a temperamental old heating system. We now think this was wonderfully lucky. The land and much of the garden have been sold instead, to be restored to new glory by someone with the resources to make this possible, but the actual house is being lived in by a sixth generation of the family and once again echoes with the happy sound of children playing. However, I am over-running my story.

With the house up for sale, and a move imminent, we had to think of a new solution for my mother. We found a delightful flat for her in the converted stable block of a lovely old house that had been turned into a nursing home. It gave her the independence she valued so much, but with nursing care immediately available and meals cooked if she wanted, though she had her own small kitchen. It seemed – to us – ideal, but not to her.

Since my father had died I looked in on her every day, usually twice, and she felt very threatened by the idea of losing this daily contact. Her struggle for dominance, and dislike of not being fully in command, had always had its hilarious side: whenever she came to eat with us, especially if our family were staying, she would assert her independence in curious ways. She always brought her own little jug of cream or would arrive – although well aware that a place would have been laid for her – clutching her own plates, knives and forks, to the particular amusement of my sons-in-law, who treasured stories about her.

Now she would be fifteen miles away.

At nearly ninety, it was a huge upheaval for her to face. I was wretchedly afraid that the disruption in my life might sound the death knell for hers, but my mother's courage was never in question. She would have been a splendid choice to have standing next to you to face a firing-squad – her backbone would have been ramrod straight.

Though capable of huge generosity on occasion, she had never been one to part with possessions at anyone else's suggestion – and this tenacious hold went equally for daughters or endless cardboard boxes of old Christmas cards. She was a hoarder on a truly epic scale. My brother came down to help me move her to her new flat. We shall neither of us forget it.

As it turned out, the move gave my mother and me, for nearly two years, an easier relationship than we'd had since my childhood. I did my best to visit her twice a week, and she would come to me, daringly cutting in at the various roundabouts that divided us, and hogging the middle of the road as she had been taught to do by my grandfather's coachman-turned-chauffeur in her youth: 'Never allow yourself to be pushed into the verge, Miss Janet.' She never did.

I had first seen my new house at the beginning of March, but it did not become mine till September. I enormously enjoyed doing it up, and never lost that first conviction that I had made the right decision, but there was a feeling of unreality about those last months at Arthington. I could hardly believe that I was about to take a pair of scissors to a tie which bound me so closely to Charlie and our life together. There were days when I could hardly bear it either. I moved house just before Christmas, eighteen months after Charlie's death.

The actual move was awful. Belinda and Susannah came to help, and because we are such boon companions, they managed to turn a time of darkness into one of showers with bright intervals. I knew how sad it felt for them to see their childhood home being dismantled, but they were wonderfully cheerful in front of me. Arthington looked increasingly sad and shabby, and I found myself walking about telling the house I was sorry to have failed it. It was like parting from a lover.

During my last day there, I crept upstairs, exhausted, to escape the packing up for a bit and lie on my bed. At that moment, for a short time, I felt I never wished to get up again. Then the removal men came to take the bed, so I had to stir myself. It was just as well.

There is a trapdoor in the ceiling of my new spare bedroom which leads to a useful loft. That first night was unbelievably wild and windy, and we realized why the house is called West Winds. In the small hours of the morning I heard a terrific crash followed by two blood-curdling shrieks. The trapdoor had blown open and the ladder attached to it had whooshed down, narrowly missing the two beds. The dawn saw the three of us drinking tea in my new kitchen, and I experienced for the first time the bliss of just being able to press the central heating button and hear the boiler roar into action. The house was warm in no time. I am still in love with that heating button. The novelty has not worn off in two years – but I have gone soft and am no longer such a hardy plant as I used to be.

It can be exciting to see one's possessions in a different setting. There were some nice surprises. My choice of what pictures and furniture I took, partly sentimental, also had to be dictated by size: some things actually looked better in their new and smaller setting, and I saw them with a fresh eye. It seemed symbolic.

Will and Alice and my mother came to me for Christmas, and this time, having Christmas in my new house was similar to buttering the paws of a cat. It made the house into a home. I had taken an important step on the road to recovery.

It was not till the New Year that the reality of my new life hit me. This was the time that I finally faced the fact that my old way of life had gone. Though all my children were grown-up, Arthington had still been very much a centre of family life, so there was something of the empty-nest syndrome to be accepted too.

Shortly before Charlie died he had made me promise that when I was left on my own I would try to make something of my writing.

I can't remember a time when I haven't tried to write

poetry. Poetry has been famously described as 'emotion recollected in tranquillity'. Not for me it isn't. Mine is usually emotion recollected in anguish – it is my own personal scream-therapy, and for me a marvellous outlet in times of great stress. It is one of the things that really helped me. I believe counsellors are told to help their client 'give their sorrow words'. I suppose this is how I do it for myself.

Last year, during a week on the island of Iona, I was persuaded to take a session on 'using writing to get in touch with your feelings'. I had never done this before, and felt very unqualified to do so, but it had some amazing results. I got everyone to write, for up to six minutes, a vivid early recollection. My only stipulations were that they should use the present tense, not stop to think and keep writing. Then those who felt brave enough shared the results. Some extraordinarily vivid and moving memories came out, and several people said they had released things which had been bottled up for years. Anyone can try this: you do not need a class.

My earliest efforts at poems as a small child were not bad considering my age, but the growing-up ones were pretty horrendous: awful hybrid mixtures, sort of crosses between Patience Strong and bad attempts to reproduce Tennyson. However, I had my first published poem in the *Sunday Times* when I was only seventeen – real beginner's luck. I stopped writing poems through the child-bearing years. Really creative people can do both, but what spark I have has always been rather feeble. I wrote doggerel for school concerts and light-hearted verses for family occasions – I've always been able to do that – but nothing more serious. In my thirties, I suddenly started again, and some of my poems were published in magazines; then I got withered by rejection slips (I didn't realize other people got them too), and crept back into my crab-shell. I didn't stop writing, but I stopped sending them out for years. Then some chance encouragement and invaluable criticism set me off again.

Charlie was delighted. He had always said I ought to get back to it, though he claimed to be tone deaf to the music of words. I began to get acceptances again. When my first small volume of poems was published in 1990 by the National Poetry Foundation, a registered charity and small poetry publisher, Charlie was very pleased and took great pride in it – so long as he didn't have to read them. I also tried my hand at a novel – just for fun and to see if I could do it. It seemed that I couldn't. It was firmly rejected. I was not surprised, but I'd had fun trying. I stuck it in a drawer and forgot about it.

In the New Year of 1993, having done my statutory widow's move and shed many of the burdens that had previously kept me busy, I realized that there was now nothing to stop me – except myself. Each morning I got up full of good intentions to try and write something – anything would have done. Each night I would go to bed not having written a word. As always with me, a fear of failure played its part in this feebleness. I felt low and demoralized, and quite frightened too. There is nothing like living alone – really alone – to bring you face to face with yourself. The thought of being incarcerated from now on with this dreary, self-pitying non-starter was alarming: I did not like myself at all. Any initiative seemed to have gone AWOL.

In some ways I found the second year of bereavement more difficult than the first. Anniversaries can be difficult – and remain so – but I had got over the first one. The drama is over and a sort of dreariness sets in. Also you realize that it is time to relinquish that seductively cosseting starring role as new widow.

Then I had a stroke of luck. I saw an article on correspondence courses in journalism, and sent for details. I thought it might jump-start me into some sort of action, so I signed on.

The result of this course, and the advice of the tutor assigned to me, was that I rewrote the dud novel, changing the plot and bearing a lot of criticism in mind. A year later it was accepted for publication. I cannot describe what it did for my self-respect to have this boost at that particular moment. It has given new purpose to my life, extended my horizons – and I still feel I have to pinch myself to prove I'm not dreaming and won't wake up and find it's not true. I passionately longed for Charlie to know. When the first copies of my novel arrived on my doorstep – a thrilling moment for any author – I first of all felt totally euphoric. Then I cried and cried because he was not there to share that moment with me.

I'm glad my mother lived to know it was accepted. In the past she'd been baffled by my efforts to get my work accepted; not about the actual writing – which she regarded as a nice little hobby – but about this extraordinary wish to 'go public'. She couldn't understand why I needed to know that someone else considered my writing good enough to warrant risking financial outlay on it. However, once both my two small collections of poetry were actually published, she was thrilled and bought copies for all her friends. Having declined, several years before, to read the novel in its original form, she agreed to read the new, accepted version, in manuscript. I don't think she expected to like it but, in fact, she did – to our mutual pleasure. Sadly she didn't live to see it in book form.

There is no doubt that having a novel published gave me great joy and a tremendous sense of achievement; it has greatly helped me to come to terms with a new lifestyle and given me a new sense of myself as a person in my own right, and not just as the leftover one of a partnership. I have been lucky, but I don't think it matters what one does – success is not the criterion: pursuing a special personal interest is the important thing – enjoyment is important in itself – and helps with the difficult new test of 'flying solo'.

My mother's last two years were happy ones for our relationship together, and a lot of what Elisabeth Kübler-Ross calls 'unfinished business' between us was resolved. Had it not been so, I think I would have had much greater problems with myself when she died. Our love for each other had never been in question, and though we respected each other's very different strengths, we often clashed. I owe my wonderful relationship with my own daughters to my mother: because I'd had such a struggle to fly the nest and try my wings, I learnt the value of being more open-handed, and have reaped huge benefit from this. I sometimes felt that the close friendship they share with me must have been hard for my mother to witness. I often felt the need to keep a distance between us in case she gobbled me up again – and it became a habit.

Susannah gave us a wonderful Christmas that year, a great contrast to the lonely one two years before. The excitement of the children gave me back its special magic. It was to be my mother's last but, always brilliant with the very young, we have wonderful memories of her playing with Freddie. She spent much of the time with her feet up on the drawing-room sofa, cast in the role of Baby Jesus. Freddie played all the other more energetic roles in the drama. He must have been the only person ever to get my mother to put her feet up voluntarily.

On New Year's Eve we had the joy and excitement of the arrival of Octavia, Will and Alice's first baby. I have a touching photograph of my mother holding her: one life so very new, the other about to end.

Mum had always been asthmatic, and there had been two spells in hospital with breathing problems in the last few years, so when she was taken into the Duchy Hospital in Harrogate with a chest infection, some weeks before her ninety-first birthday, we did not necessarily think it heralded the end. Since the first abortive Christmas trip after Charlie died, I had managed to get her up to Scotland twice, once for the wedding of my brother's youngest daughter, and the next time for her own ninetieth birthday celebrations.

Returning from this last junket, my car had broken down, which involved a long wait before being towed behind an AA van for a nerve-racking twenty-seven-mile trip to Penrith – during which the AA van ran out of petrol – followed by another long wait and eventual return home with my car on the back of a transporter, and my mother, two dogs and myself squashed in the front with the driver. What should have been a five-hour drive, took over twelve hours. It was a nightmare day and I was very worried about the effect this might have on her.

'Don't worry, darling. I've loved every minute of it. It's the most exciting adventure I've had for ages!' she said. This was my mother at her endearing, indomitable best; the thing that made her irresistible – when one wasn't feeling like murdering her.

The heart drugs she was having made her terribly sick, so it was decided to stop them, which was a great relief to her. She immediately felt much better.

I had promised to stand in for Belinda and Charles at an event at Arabella's school, and go on to London with Susannah the following day for Brian Johnston's memorial service in Westminster Abbey. I was terribly anxious to attend this, not only for Charlie's sake, but also to show support for Pauline. All through the years of Charlie's illness, Brian had rung him up every two or three weeks from all over the place to enquire how he was and cheer him up. They made each other laugh inordinately at the most frightful jokes. After Charlie died Brian continued to do the same for me until his own sad and sudden collapse. It is that kind of friendship that means so much in bereavement. He and Pauline had been to stay in my new house for the Headingly Test Match, as they had always done for so many years at Arthington.

I didn't know what to do, but my mother, who so adored Arabella, was desperate for me to go. 'I couldn't bear it if you let that little girl down on my account,' she said. Because she was feeling so much better, I decided at any rate to go to Arabella and then see how things were. I rang the hospital early in the morning, before setting off, and all was well – my mother had had a good night.

After the school event I drove back to Susannah in Derbyshire and rang the hospital. The Sister said my mother was fine. When I spoke to her myself, her voice sounded stronger than it had done for weeks: she was full of chat. I thought it would be safe to stay the night with Susannah, go down to Brian's service together on the early train, and then go back to Yorkshire.

'I'll see you tomorrow evening, Mum,' I said, and went

to bed very relieved to hear her so happy. It was a shock when the hospital rang an hour later to say she had died.

I feel that at some level there is a choice about the time of death. Naturally I am not speaking of accidental death. Elisabeth Kübler-Ross tells us how often dying children go at the one moment when parents, who have been constantly at their bedside, are momentarily absent. To anguished parents this can bring even greater distress, but she believes that sometimes it is only when the people they love most are absent that the dying can 'let go'. If I had not read a good deal about this, I think I might have been very upset that my mother died when I was away. As it was, I felt sure that it is how she wanted it.

The week before, I had been holding her hand when she was feeling nauseous and miserable, and she had said, 'You've had too much of sick-rooms. I had so hoped to spare you all this.' I know she would like to have done so too, but I told her truthfully that it was more important for me to share with her than be shut out. Her last words to me as I kissed her goodnight before my trip south were, 'You are my lynchpin.' This was a far from typical utterance, and all the more poignant for that. I cried all the way home. As with Nan, all those years before, it is a wonderful goodbye to look back on.

Susannah and I did not go to Brian's service. We drove early next morning straight to the hospital. They had promised to keep my mother in her bed if we could get there early. We were so grateful to them for this. It made such a difference to us to be able to say our private farewell in her room. She looked unusually peaceful – and miles away. That fiercely loving, strong-willed, energetic spirit had gone. We were both struck too by how tiny and strangely vulnerable she looked. She always had been small, but somehow her personality was so large that we had never thought about it.

We discovered later that she had spoken to nearly all her nearest and dearest in the few hours before she died. She had a long and cheerful call with my brother. She had listened to *Songs of Praise* on the television, which she always loved, and then rang her sister to say what a particularly good one it had been. They had sung 'The day thou gavest, Lord, is ended'. 'My favourite hymn – I should like that at my funeral,' she told my aunt. We would not have known this otherwise.

Unlike Charlie, whose health had declined over such a long period, my mother had been firing on all cylinders till the end, and had been ill only for a few weeks. It is a comfort to know that someone has had a long and good life, but the fact of old age itself doesn't stop you grieving for someone. Many people said, 'Oh well, she had a good innings, you can't be sad.' I knew what they meant, but if you love someone you *are* sad when they are no longer there. Also the loss of a parent takes one's childhood with it. Funnily enough, just the other day, while talking on the telephone to a stranger about buying a puppy, she apologized to me for not having returned my call sooner. 'We've just lost my mother-in-law,' she said, 'and it's really thrown me. People seem to think that because she was over eighty we shouldn't mind.' I knew what she meant.

When my brother and sister-in-law arrived, we collected my mother's things from the hospital. 'I suppose we ought to look in her bag in case there's anything important,' David said. Then he handed me a piece of paper. It was a half-filled-in application form for a new railcard. 'Read that,' he said. In answer to the rather surprising question, 'What are your hobbies and interests?' my mother had written *LIVING!* It says much about her outlook. We laughed and cried.

It took my mother's death to tip me over an edge. Mum's funeral at Arthington brought back all the memories of Charlie's funeral. The following week I went up to Scotland to visit Belinda – and got flu. Whether it was the after-effects of this, my mother's death, the consequent reopening of wounds about Charlie or a mixture of the three, I don't know, but two months later I landed in my doctor's surgery seeking medical help.

Outwardly things were going amazingly well for me. My first novel was finished and accepted, I was halfway through writing my second one. Thanks to help from family and friends I had started on a new life and felt I should be relishing this upward curve, not sinking into a trough of despair *now* – but life had lost its sparkle. Everything was a physical effort, the smallest decisions seemed threatening, and I had a constant sense of inner panic. Insomnia, my old enemy, was vicious. I could put on an outward show of cheerfulness, and none of this prevented me from carrying on with life, but the effort involved alarmed me. Nowadays, if I hear people saying of someone who has been bereaved, 'Oh, they're wonderful – coping splendidly', I wonder what they feel like inside when the curtains are drawn and there is no one else to see. Everyone expects the newly bereaved to need a lot of help, but several people have commented to me that it can be almost as difficult, though in a different way, later on when the need for support is less obvious. We are anxious not to disappoint friends and family who have been so kind and patient, and perhaps we put unnecessary pressure on ourselves to appear cheerful at all times.

I certainly felt terribly ashamed that I seemed incapable of enjoying all the luck that had recently come my way. I had often felt low and sad before, but there had been many reasons for it then, and this was different. It was not welcome to hear the doctor say I had clinical depression – I who perhaps secretly rather prided myself on being able to cope – and that he wanted to put me on anti-depressants.

I hated taking those pills. I hated the spaced-out feeling they gave me, the weight gain and sensation of being blown up. I think after the first days of unpleasant side-effects had worn off a bit, I expected to feel instantly wonderful, but it was much more gradual. However, after a couple of months I realized that, almost without noticing it, I was taking ordinary decisions again without getting the shakes; that I was spending less time sitting hopelessly in front of my word processor without actually writing anything; and that the sun was beginning to shine for me again. I suggested to the doctor that I came off the pills, but he was insistent it was too soon.

That September I had a car crash. Luckily it wasn't my fault and there was no question of prosecution, but my car was a write-off and I was badly shocked and bruised. Ironically I had been on my way to try and cheer up my aunt in Derbyshire, herself low after my mother's death and feeling very much 'next in line'. I was then going on to stay with Susannah. The other driver involved, whose car was still usable, had rung the police on my mobile telephone and been given permission to leave the scene and collect his children, who would otherwise have been stranded, but the police mistook his instructions as to my whereabouts, and I was trapped in my car for an hour and a half before they found me.

Hearing the officer describe me into his telephone as 'an elderly lady in a severe state of shock' was a nasty shock in itself. Amazing as it may seem to anyone younger, at just turned sixty I had never thought of myself in this light before. There were freak thunderstorms going on. My dogs became instantly sodden on being transferred to the police car and soaked the back seat, but the police were very sweet about it. Waterlogged dogs may be better than drunks being sick, I suppose.

I declined suggestions that I should go to hospital, and Susannah drove fifty miles in deluging rain to collect me from the police station. Three-year-old Freddie, whom she'd had to scoop from bed in his pyjamas, thought it a thrilling adventure. Sue swears that when she arrived she could hear me, through still clattering teeth, discussing the marital problems of the young policeman who'd rescued me. I had the tea – and he got the sympathy!

The pain was beginning to strike, and I couldn't straighten up, but they got me into her car. Freddie was heard telling someone next day, 'Me and Mummy often have to collect Granny from police stations at night when she can't walk properly.'

Out of such slight inaccuracies myths are born.

I stayed at Susannah's for a week and it was a wonderful convalescence – to be told by her doctor to stay in bed and do nothing but rest for at least a week was in some ways just what I needed. Illness or accident can give us permission to take time out without feeling guilty. Perhaps this is why the newly bereaved so often fall prey to infection. The only snag in this case was that my cracked sternum made laughing excruciatingly painful, and, as always in the company of my family, trivial things seemed enormously funny.

It might be worth mentioning here the experience of a younger friend of mine whose husband had been instantly killed in a car crash on a motorway some years before. She herself was badly hurt in the accident, was in hospital for several weeks and then confined to a wheelchair for several more. A normally very active and busy person, she told me that she felt those weeks of forced inactivity had helped her to come to terms with the awful shock and desolation quicker than if she'd been rushing about smothering her pain in a cloak of frenetic activity. Stuck in a wheelchair she had nothing to do but grieve.

I am not, however, recommending car crashes as therapy.

Recently, a Jewish friend of mine, who had been widowed, told me about the custom of Sitting Shivar, the aim of which is to allow the bereaved person to mourn properly, and for other people to be able to acknowledge the bereavement and make their condolences. For the first seven days all their friends and acquaintances visit them and share their grief. They are not allowed to lift a finger to do anything, and are totally surrounded by caring and protection. I have to say I don't think I would feel drawn to anything as formal as this, but perhaps most of us have too few formulas for dealing with loss.

Though I could not have avoided my particular accident, it did make me wonder if my reactions were slowed up by the anti-depressant pills, and at the end of October, after four months, I persuaded the doctor to let me give them up gradually. I would not have been stupid enough to do so without his permission, but it was a huge relief when he agreed – albeit with slight reluctance. I think they did the trick, however, and perhaps it was good for me to have to acknowledge that I had needed help.

My son teases me about the pearls of advice he says I

always have ready in my pocket for other people. I am not always so good at wearing them myself.

I started this book in Corfu, but, of course, it has taken me more than a fortnight's holiday to get this far. In any case, the sea, the sun, and the pleasure of my family's company soon beguiled me, and what began as a resolve to write every morning soon went the way of most of my good resolutions.

So where am I now? On the whole in a very good place. I know I am exceedingly fortunate.

I have an enormous amount of fun. I have wonderful friends, both old and new; I have a growing band of grand-children who are a delight; I have a small house which I love, and – wonder of wonders – I have a career. When Geordie, Belinda's youngest son, was seven, he described me to some-one as 'my wild writing Granny', a title I treasure.

After the publication of my first novel, a profile on me in a newspaper quoted me as saying how lucky I felt to have started a new career at this late stage in my life, and that I hoped it might encourage others in the same situation to feel that, because life has changed, it is by no means over and that it is possible to start again. To my astonishment, this produced quite a spate of letters from complete strangers to say it had given them courage. It was this, more than anything, that made me agree to try to write this book.

I had mentioned my feelings of relief that when Charlie died, his suffering was over. One woman wrote touchingly to say that this had helped her not to feel guilty because she was glad about her own husband's death after a similar long haul. She has taken up art again and started to drive a car. She illustrated her letter with a branch of plum blossom, done with a Chinese brush pen – a symbol of hope, she said.

'My feeling is that a crushing weight of fear and worry has been lifted. I have grieved for the lovely man he once was, but I don't want to remember the almost fleshless stranger he had become.' I was very moved by this and other letters.

Of course loneliness remains. There is a longing for a loving companion, but definitely not at any price. For me having no one is infinitely better than having the wrong person. I always come back to that. I do not want to submerge my new life in someone else's, perhaps to uproot, just when I've got over the painful pulling up of old roots and have started to put down new ones, which are wriggling their binding little shoots into fresh soil. Perhaps it is cowardly, but I would be terrified of giving so much love a second time and risking loss again.

One of the things that used to make me grind my teeth when I was newly widowed was when well-meaning sympathizers said, 'You still look quite young for your age – you might even marry again', as though I might con some luckless male about my shelf-life, as though remarriage offered the only possible way of happiness for someone as apparently unqualified to do anything else as I seemed.

However, old habits die hard, and in my exciting new life I find it very difficult to discipline myself to write as a routine. All my life I have been used to the discipline of my existence coming from someone else's needs or wishes. This, for me, is an easier way than having to draw all the motivation for any action from myself. I am both amazed and enchanted by my new career – and absolutely terrified of it.

The fear of failure, deeply ingrained in me, and with it the temptation not to try, flickers like a constant shadow on my wall. Sometimes I can manage to ignore it, sometimes not, but it is always there.

I recently heard a wonderful writer interviewed on the radio and was astonished (and comforted) to hear her admitting to so many of my own hang-ups: the terror of failing, the lack of trust in her gift, the feeling of being uneducated – so much so in my case that I have always felt a fear of being found wanting by people who expect me to be both more knowledgeable and more intelligent than I really am. She obviously had an unconventional early education – or lack of one – too. I am grateful that mine has prevented me from being too typecast, too trapped in any particular mould, but it has also left me with an undisciplined mind and the lurking fear of feeling myself an outsider, on the wrong side of a door. I may not wish to go through any particular door, but it can be draughty outside on the mat.

Unlike her, I never felt myself unloved as a child by either parent – far from it – my problem was more one of over-protection, but I certainly felt that what few talents I had were, not exactly of no account, but certainly not to be taken seriously: more like the amusing toy of a beloved child than anything that could be useful for life, let alone a career. All the conditioning of my youth was not to put myself forward.

Perhaps I have gone overboard the other way now!

Of course there are things I still miss – perhaps I always will. I miss the stimulation that two very different minds and temperaments brought to each other. I miss Charlie's keen brain and encyclopaedic fund of general knowledge. I miss doing *The Times* crossword together. This has been a surprising casualty. We used to do it regularly, right to the end of his life, and though he probably had the edge over me, I still made a big contribution. Now I can't do it. It seems very curious. I have occasionally tried and been so disgusted by my performance that I've given up: it's too depressing.

Sometimes I miss unlikely things that would make Charlie laugh: through him I had access to knowledge that I would never bother to acquire for myself. For instance, the summer following his death, I was amazed to find I had no idea what horse had won the Derby. It used to be a joke to him that I could read my book through sporting programmes on television and not hear a word – but perhaps more information filtered through than we realized. I had never thought of reading as being a companionable occupation, but now that I live alone, and would expect to be able to lose myself in my book, I often feel so acutely conscious of the empty chair on the other side of the fireplace that I can't concentrate. I tend to go to bed early and read there instead, sometimes till the small hours, rather than sit downstairs aware of the space that no one else can fill.

Above all, I suppose I miss being first with someone. This seems an awful egoistical admission when I still have so much love from my family. I am lucky ever to have been greatly loved at all – perhaps the greatest privilege anyone can have in life – but if you have once had something wonderful, then you miss it when it is gone.

During the last years of Charlie's illness, I sometimes had to take difficult decisions because he hadn't got the energy to do so. For his sake I was able to do this. Now I often find the smallest things almost impossible to resolve. For instance, I have received and enjoyed an enormous amount of hospitality lately, but asking anyone back can be a major issue. I find this odd. I used to love entertaining, and fancied myself as a good and imaginative cook who coped with a household which was usually humming with people.

Now the thought of picking up the telephone to initiate a plan or issue an invitation, even to friends I know well, can seem infinitely threatening. I toy with the idea and postpone action for days, often indefinitely.

At Arthington, supported by a husband and surrounded by family, I suppose I felt I had something outside of myself to offer. Now there is just me – and that does not seem enough. This has got a little easier as time goes by, and I am getting braver, but it is still a problem. A friend has suggested that it could be just laziness!

Like most married couples, Charlie and I could infuriate each other at times. Hidden emotion was very much his forte, and in our early years I sometimes longed for the great romantic speech from him, and yet occasionally over the years, he would write the most wonderful love letter, saying all and more than I could ever hope for. These letters usually came completely out of the blue and seldom appeared at obvious times like anniversaries. They were all the more precious: they still are. When he died, I had this wild, mad conviction that he would have left such a letter for me knocking around somewhere, summing up all that our life together had meant. I drew a blank in his desk, but since Charlie had even less of a filing-cabinet mentality than I have, this was no particular surprise.

Then I took the house apart in a frenzy of anguished searching.

Though it would have been quite in character for Charlie to have done something like this, over the last few years the physical act of writing had become extremely difficult for him, and in the last months of his life, utterly impossible. Of course, I found nothing. It was a crazy, irrational fixation, born of a longing to hang on to some sort of communication from him. At the time, I never told anyone about this desperate hope of mine. I know there will be no more love letters now.

Through all my ups and downs, what has never deserted me for long has been the capacity to enjoy life as a whole. Nobody can escape some bereavement and grief in this life. Perhaps happiness is something we partly make ourselves, but it is also a precious gift. I have been given a large share of it – and I am very grateful.

This is the poem that was triggered by the discovery of Charlie's single glove in the pocket of his Puffa jacket. I had always wanted to try my hand at writing a villanelle.

Left-hand Gloves
(A Villanelle)

My cupboard has a shelf of left-hand gloves
whose partners have been lost or thrown away:
the point of keeping them is hard to prove.

Though our twined fingers locked so close in love,
I saw your gauntlet buried yesterday.
Is there a use for one odd left-hand glove?

Your hand has gone that made our right glove move:
the glove became too thin for it to stay.
The point of keeping mine is hard to prove.

Two-handed, a bright tapestry we wove:
now I must seek a different role to play
and find a use for just one left-hand glove.

I stretch my hand: is yours below, above?
And can you hear when I cry out and say,
'The point of life alone seems hard to prove'?

Your spirit's flown the body it once drove,
to find a subtler one, and I must pray
that I can find a use for one left glove –
although just now the point seems hard to prove.

Just as I finished writing this book, the eighteen-year-old daughter of some great friends was killed in a tragic and bizarre accident in Africa. All their friends were overwhelmed with longing to be able to wave a magic wand for this warm and close family and take their anguish away – but, of course, we can't. They have asked me to include this poem which I wrote for them in memory of Laura.

All We Can Do

For Robert and Rosie – in memory of Laura

No words can comfort:
all we can do
is share your north-face
route with you.

No one can take
your pain away
or cut bereavement's
journey short.
Perhaps you would
not want them to
– your grief is all
that's left to you
of one, so loved,
who could not stay.

All we can do
is walk with you,
and try to match
our steps to yours.
Friends do not need
acknowledgement:
don't waste your strength
to make response;
just keep on walking
day by day.

But let us share
that cold road too
– to walk a little
way with you.

Part Five

I am conscious, in telling the story of Charlie's long illness, that I had, as it were, a slow puncture to cope with. Though I would not wish on anyone the torment of seeing the person they love most suffer over a long period, I am well aware that other people have had to cope with losses that are more like a horrendous burst tyre on the motorway – a sudden cutting off of a husband, wife or child in his or her prime that is not only an overwhelming loss but a truly appalling shock.

Such a disaster overtook Susan and her children, when her husband, David, tried to move a fallen power line and was instantly electrocuted. Much of my grieving was done in the run-up to Charlie's death: all of hers after the event. Luckily we cannot weigh miseries in a balance and get an exact reading of their impact, but what she had to cope with is terrible by any standard.

I went to see Susan in her house near Oxford, the house she and David had bought together as a country retreat, and where the accident happened. David was a brilliant and much-admired political journalist at the height of his career.

Before I visited Susan I had read many of David's obituaries and talked to two people who knew him. Clearly he was outstanding, not just in his career but as a person of huge courage, both moral and physical, with a sense of humour, a capacity for friendship and a formidable mind. He caught polio while at Oxford, and for a time was totally paralysed, only able to breathe with the help of an iron lung. Though he recovered, many people felt it was this battle, first literally for survival, then to regain a normal life, that was a factor in making him the remarkable man he was.

At the time of David's death, Susan was in London, at the theatre with two of their four boys. They were having a culture blitz to introduce the boys to Shakespeare. David had been with them to *Henry IV Part I*, but had decided not to come to the second part – such apparently trivial decisions can alter the course of people's lives. When she was told, having been paged in the interval, that David was dead she could not accept it. Talking to me about her total shock, her utter disbelief, I could feel its echo still reverberating after seven years.

There had been a big storm which she had hardly been aware of in London, but in the country the electricity was off and the wires had been brought down. There was a cable across the drive. David had obviously tried to move it, but it was still live and he must have been killed instantly. It took some time before the police could get the power turned off and his body moved to the nearest hospital, though there was never any question of resuscitation.

Susan went to the chapel of rest at the hospital and saw David, and then had his body brought nearer home. For the next four days she spent a lot of time sitting by him, holding his hand, talking and talking to him. She felt terribly angry that there had been no chance to say goodbye to him. All the children saw him, and would come in and out, then perhaps the younger ones would go and play in the garden for a bit. Susan feels strongly that it is important, even for young children, to be able to see the body if possible, to make their farewells and to attend the funeral. She thinks it helps to bring home the reality of what has happened, and therefore start the long but necessary process of coming to terms with it.

We talked together on the day the news had come through of the probable death of the young climber Alison Hargreaves on K2, in Pakistan. Her body may never be found, her family may never know exactly what happened, and we both felt this awful doubt must make the grieving process even more difficult. To be presented with the loss but not the certainty, not the how and where of it, leaving chinks of hope open for days, must delay facing the grim truth. Many people in the war whose relatives were reported 'Missing, believed killed' must have had to cope with this anguish. Later I shall quote a chilling example of what can happen in an extreme case of denial – the frightful consequence of failure to accept a loss.

Since I first wrote this, we have seen the television film of Alison's husband taking their two small children on a pilgrimage to see 'Mummy's last mountain' and witnessed their efforts to come to terms with her death.

When someone dies, in whatever way, the first few days are incredibly busy. There is a funeral service to plan, forms to be filled in; the death has to be registered. There are constant, small, exhausting decisions to be taken. Susan remembers vividly finding it weird, almost unbelievable that the social side of life could creep in – that close friends and relations who came back to the house for tea after the funeral could chat together and even laugh, when to her the sky seemed to have gone completely black, such a bright light had been extinguished. This struck a dreadfully discordant note for her.

Susan kept a diary for the first two years after David died. I envy her that. I sometimes wish I had access to the raw feelings of my worst times. I think I remember them vividly, but there must be things I have forgotten or that have got overlaid by other, later emotions. My children have reminded me of things that had completely slipped out of my mind.

Susan found it astonishing that after only three months some people were expecting her – or she felt that they were – to lead a normal life again. This was so different from my own experience. I felt after three months that perhaps it was beginning to be possible to lead a normal life for the first time in years.

She divides her period of mourning into several different stages: the first devastated week with all its shock and unreality, then the first three months, which she described as just an agony of trying to cope, even to exist. Later came the raw grief, followed by the awful slow realization that this is how life is going to be from now on. After that she found there was a stage when she almost wanted to conjure some of that raw grief back, as a way of keeping contact with David. I know that feeling too, and many other people have commented on it. 'Don't try to take my grief away – it's all I've got left,' screamed one anguished woman, whose child had died, to would-be comforters, and this cry has been used as the title of a book on the subject of bereavement. Letting go of grief can be extremely difficult, not only as a way of keeping contact with the departed, but also as a prop for dealing with life. It is disconcertingly easy to get used to special consideration. Eventually, in order to get on with life, we do have to learn to let our grief go to some degree, but there are no right rules about timing. What we want to do is to keep the love and good memories alive but not to allow ourselves to get trapped in our sorrow like a fly in amber.

For most people it is incredibly hard to face the many decisions which now have to be taken alone. Susan says she was always trying to hear David's voice and was always talking to him in her head, asking questions about what she should do about the family or work – all the things they used to discuss together.

She felt she was walking through a terribly arid and lonely desert, stretching ahead beyond where her eye could see. Despite enormous love and support from friends, and however close one's friends and family may be, no one can ever understand exactly the tight weave of someone else's intimate relationship. One can be haunted by the fear of responsibility for the death, by the hopeless question, 'If I had been a better person, done this or that differently, might the death not have happened?' Of course, this is irrational, but grief has very little to do with being rational, and the weirdest obsessions can take root and exert a terrible power. My conviction that Charlie must have left me a last letter before he died, even though he could no longer wield a pen, was such an obsession.

In Jill Truman's moving book *Letter to My Husband*, she too felt that by her occasional irritated 'wish you were dead' feelings over the years – which most of us feel for our nearest and dearest at some time – she might have somehow contributed to causing her husband's death: 'Suddenly, unreasonably, I felt I was responsible for your death, and began to sob and cried out loud – a madness which passed quite quickly. What causes it? Perhaps . . . because sometimes when you were driving me mad, I wished you would just drop dead?'

One of the key losses for a widow or widower, is the feeling that the one person for whom we came first is gone. That we can no longer hold out a hand (no matter what disagreements may have taken place) and know that there will be another hand – *the* other hand – to come halfway to reach out and clasp it. I thought of Tennyson's words: 'But O for the touch of a vanish'd hand,/And the sound of a voice that is still!'

After I had moved from Arthington, in a fit of desolation and an absolute longing to hear Charlie's voice, I once went and yelled his name aloud to the wind on a wild winter's day. Luckily there was no one near to hear or see such over-dramatic behaviour. I have included the poem that resulted from this episode at the beginning of this book.

For many widows, myself included, coping with the business side of life – the finances – is a tedious burden, something husbands had always dealt with. I once had a school report which said, 'Figures appear to have no meaning for Mary', so I suspect I was a lot worse at it than Susan was. As I'm a great deal less efficient and organized, I was comforted to find that she had found this hard too – an example of how reassuring it can be to find one's problems are experienced by others, the main object in writing and publishing this book.

I think this particular difficulty, which many widows face and find tough, of coping with the financial side of life, may be less of a problem in the future as so many more young women have careers and are much more in charge of their own lives than a previous generation like mine.

Unlike Susan, I had never had a career, but she and I

both felt lucky that we had always had a degree of independence and done things outside the home. In my case, among other things, I had been a magistrate, on the governing body of a large girls' school and, owing to Charlie's illness, had increasingly had to learn to do certain things on my own. For those women who have put their entire strength and devotion into family life, having to pick up the reins of independence must be extra tough.

Because this is a personal look at loss, this book is written from the perspective of a woman, but for men whose wives have made a career of looking after them and always kept the domestic life flowing, the home must suddenly seem a very bleak place. I admire men who learn to cook and care for both children and themselves every bit as much as I admire women who have to go out to work for the first time.

If someone is seized in a violent and totally unexpected way, there is no time to put one's mental and emotional house in order, but because some of us have had long preparation it does not automatically mean we get things right. To resent the person you love most in the world for going on living and putting one through such agony can bring its own burden of miserable guilt. A great friend of mine who nursed her much-loved husband through a long illness when she was still a young woman with small children remembers weeping desperately to him and saying, 'I wish you'd either get better *or die.*' He replied, 'I'm doing my best.' He died, aged forty-four, after a ten-year battle with kidney disease. She told me this when I was in the middle of my own long slog and I found it deeply reassuring. I never actually said the same words to Charlie, but I might well have done, and I often felt like it.

When I was a child, I remember thinking the exhortation in the hymn to 'Live each day as if 'twere thy last' was incredibly dull and stuffy. What spontaneity and fun would be removed if we were always treading so cautiously in our relationships, behaving so dreadfully well? Nevertheless, guilt is a very real, common and painful part of bereavement. Often it is an illogical guilt just for being the one who is left alive. We feel less worthy than the one who has gone.

Like me, Susan had experienced the pain of losing a baby – a little girl, who only lived a few hours. Because Susan has no religious faith herself, does not believe in God, or any survival after death, any trite phrases such as, 'I expect he is often with you in spirit', are not only meaningless, but perhaps offensive. Because I do believe in a survival of consciousness after death (a bit wavery sometimes!) I felt her courage was of a bleaker, tougher kind than mine. I came away from my evening with Susan lost in admiration at her courage – and quite humbled.

I was interested in Susan's views about the importance of taking on board the finality of death and her strong feelings that it is important for children not to be over-protected from the rites and ceremonies that surround it, including, in her case, the children seeing the body of their father. This is quite a controversial view. Once I might not have agreed with it, though now on the whole I think I do. Of course, it may not always be appropriate or possible, but here is a story of what happened in a case where death was never properly acknowledged.

There is a lot of anger in grief. Some of it has to do with fear of being out of control, of not being able to control the emotions grief brings, and because we cannot control the events which cause the grief. Anger can be good, of course: without anger we can fall victim to apathy, and allow terrible things to happen. But anger can also be destructive. I came across a terrible example of this recently. Had I read this story in a novel, I simply would not have believed it could have occurred in our own time and country – but it did.

I had been asked to give a talk on writing poetry to a women's group in a town about thirty miles from where I live. I thanked my lucky stars that it was not foggy as I took the isolated route across the moors, and was glad I had my mobile telephone in the car. I remember thinking that I would not accept any more invitations to do this sort of thing during winter. But if I had not agreed to take part in this particular evening, I would have missed meeting a remarkable woman.

During my talk I said I was prepared to bet that there would be other people present besides myself who wrote poetry to express their emotions, but who perhaps might be too shy to let anyone else see their efforts. You can paint a picture, turn a pot, do needlework or bake a perfect cake to express creative talent without exposing your inmost feelings, but to write poetry for publication can be to undress in public. There was a murmur of assent.

Afterwards the chairman asked if she could introduce one of the members to me, a woman who had recently started to write poems, and for whom what I said had touched a chord.

She was a charming person in her early sixties. She walked with a stick, and though she did not look like a young woman, she had an extraordinarily unlined face. It would have been difficult to guess her age.

This is her story. During the war, when she was eleven, her father was pronounced 'Missing, believed killed'. Her mother's reaction was that until he returned, as she convinced herself he would, their life would be put on hold. 'You will never have another birthday until your father comes home,' she told her daughter.

Unbelievable as it may seem, from that day on, the mother 'kept' her daughter at the age of eleven. No birthdays were celebrated; no books other than those suitable for a child of that age were permitted; bedtime continued at the same time; she could not choose her clothes or food; she was not allowed to handle money or know its value; she took no decisions of any kind. This mother was a much-respected member of the community and a pillar of her church. As the years went by it was accepted that the daughter was 'simple' and generally considered to be mentally retarded. The mother got credit for her devotion in looking after her daughter.

J, an abused child, slipped through the net of the education system during the war. She had little schooling. 'My mother was afraid of what I might tell anyone,' she commented. Afterwards, her state was never questioned. The one thing her mother allowed her to do was to collect dolls' houses and furniture and over the years she got together a valuable collection.

When she was seventeen she tried to stage a rebellion. She had a secret boyfriend and they decided that the only way she could get away from her 'prison' was to have a baby. Her mother killed it – she hit her daughter with a spade, late in the pregnancy. The baby, a boy, was born dead, on 1 April. Her mother laughed and said April Fool's Day was a suitable day.

J was in her fifties when her mother died. Social Services became involved: she was found to have a very high IQ. Not surprisingly, faced with independence after this extraordinary life of complete subjugation, J then had a breakdown and attempted suicide. Then she had a brain tumour. This has left her with impaired balance and she walks with a stick. I thought this was curiously ironic. The person who really had an impaired sense of balance was the mother. It seemed to me a chilling story of the way one woman's anger at her inability to control events, and her refusal to face and give outlet to her own grief, led her to ruin the life of someone else – someone whom she was supposed to love. She had lost control over events and from that time on exerted an iron control over her daughter.

I asked J if she felt bitter. She said she had done, but that her life-threatening illness had made her realize that there was much in life that was still beautiful and that she wanted the chance to experience new things. She had to sell her beloved collection of dolls' houses and the money from this has given her some slight independence. She now struggles to live alone, with support from the social services, the minister of her church and his wife, and the members of the group to whom I talked. Not surprisingly, she is still subject to depression and panic attacks. April is always a very bad time of year for her.

'You don't know what an adventure it is for me to come out to an evening like this and be accepted as an equal by other women,' she said to me. 'There are still times when the effort of doing so is too much for me to cope with.' J has recently started to write poetry, and finds it a great release.

As I drove back across that isolated road to the comfort of the home in which I now live by myself, I thought that, compared with this woman, I know very little about loneliness.

There is, for me, a delightful footnote to my meeting with this remarkable woman. When I was seeking permission to use her story, I learnt that my talk had encouraged her to send some of her work out, and she has since had a poem accepted for publication. I cannot describe what pleasure this gave me. I think she is one of the bravest people I have met. Her story gave me a sharp shake-up of priorities.

Sharing the stories of how other people have coped with tragedy in their lives has been both harrowing and inspiring.

I do not think we should be asked to *look* for good in a disaster – though wonderful people do manage to create amazingly positive things as a result of terrible grief, turn their disasters to great account and find as a bonus that it helps to ease the pain. Occasionally phoenixes rise from ashes, but I don't think anyone should be asked to expect this. For lots of us it is asking too much. As one bereaved mother said to me, 'What's good about being rung up in the small hours to hear that your brilliant son at university has skidded on black ice, hit the gritting lorry and been instantly killed?' However, this same woman went on to tell me that her greatest *help* has come from putting her energies into something creative – she, for instance, has started a business.

It is clutch-at-straws time, and if painting, gardening, cooking, writing, housework, running a business or working for a cause helps, then go for it – when, and if, you have the strength and energy to do so.

I have always loved the quotation from Psalm 84 about those 'Who going through the vale of misery use it for a well: and the pools are filled with water.' There are people who have managed to bring such water into a desert – and been saved by doing so.

Such a case is that of old friends of mine, Elizabeth and her husband, Nigel. Their only son Timothy was one of our boys at the school. I remember him as a happy, outgoing child, a very special apple in his parents' eyes. Tall, good-looking and an exceptionally good athlete, he looked set to enjoy a golden youth. Just before his first year at public school he succumbed to a throat infection which turned to nephritis. This was the start of a long battle against kidney failure. Timothy had three kidney transplants – his father donated the third one for him – and years on dialysis before he died at the age of thirty-four. His story has already been told by his mother in a moving book about his life, *Timbo: A Struggle for Survival*. Out of Timothy's struggle, and through his mother's battles on his behalf, sprang the British Kidney Patient Association which she founded in 1975, during Timothy's lifetime. This has not only changed the quality of life for many kidney patients by raising truly inspiring sums of money for their treatment and care, but has done an enormous amount in raising public awareness of kidney disease. Not everyone can have Liz's vision and determination. She is a woman of enormous charm and energy, with a talent for getting people to do things – a catalyst for action. This has not come about without much heartache and difficulty for herself and the whole family, but what she has achieved is quite remarkable. I am reminded of the wonderful words in Staunton Harold church in Leicestershire about Sir Robert Shirley, who founded the church in 1653. 'Whose singular praise it is to have done the best of things in the worst of times, and hoped them in the most calamitous.'

The father of a son who was killed in another accident involving an electric cable – he was pruning a tree with electric clippers and accidentally touched the mains wire – told me that he found some comfort in setting up a memorial fund for an endowment at his son's old school. Apart from the terrible grief, this father was harrowed by the guilt he felt because he had asked his son to help him in the garden while he was home for a weekend – a natural and commonplace request, which had an appalling consequence. It is a relief that the family have moved house and he can no longer see the tree where the tragedy occurred. He went on to say that his son's friends and contemporaries had been an enormous help to the whole family by their continued love and support, making them aware that the quality of this talented young man's life, though woefully short, had been good while it lasted and had left its mark.

One father told me of his sadness that with the death of his only son came the end of the male line in his family. This may not be a popular view today, but nevertheless it is a common and deeply felt one by many parents in similar circumstances – primitive, natural and tribal in origin – and which has nothing to do with loving or valuing a male child more than a female one. It is simply another aspect of loss and should be acknowledged as such.

The mother of a grown-up child killed in a violent accident also spoke of the unexpected amount of help from that child's contemporaries. Many of them remember the anniversary of the death, and write or ring up. This takes courage. She says she is aware that for some time she built a wall round herself, which she could not help doing, but knew she made it hard for those closest to her to reach her and give her the love they were longing to express. She says she was often 'horrid' to her nearest and dearest. This seems to be a common reaction and I think it's important to mention it. I know I did the same with my mother over Amanda. This woman feels that grief is ultimately selfish. She is sure that her child continues: it is she who has been left behind. The idea that she might seek counselling was abhorrent to her but, like me, she was lucky in her friends and family. She found great help in the wonderful anthology *All in the End is Harvest*. I too have found this book a source of strength, and have given copies to many friends who have been bereaved.

Many people have told me how unhelpful they found it when people suggested to them that they would 'get over it'. You learn to live with pain, it becomes chronic rather than acute, but you do not always get over it. Many people live with a gaping void, which may shift to the background rather than the forefront of their lives but, nevertheless, is always there. A beloved aunt of mine whose six-year-old daughter died after having her tonsils out has said the same to me. This child was profoundly deaf, but very bright, and making enormous strides in lip-reading. The tonsillectomy had nothing to do with the deafness: she haemorrhaged after the operation and there was no matching blood in the hospital. It particularly hurt my aunt when people told her that, because of the child's disability, it was 'all for the best'. Now nearly ninety, the grief over the loss of this adored little daughter is very much at the front of her mind again. I was made godmother to this child when I was eleven, and took my duties tremendously seriously. I was seventeen when she died, and it was the first time I had encountered the fact that death is no respecter of age. It made a lasting impression on me.

Yorkshire neighbours and friends of ours, Juliet and James, were about to catch a train to London when they were called for on the Tannoy at York station and asked to go immediately to the station master's office. They knew at once that something awful must have happened. They were met by a policeman and told, 'Your daughter and son-in-law have been killed in a car crash.' I asked if it had taken time for this horrifying news to sink in, but Juliet said no. Unlike Susan, she had believed it instantly.

Lottie and Mark were both talented artists, who had each had paintings exhibited. They had jointly started a school of art in Edinburgh which was flourishing, and into which they had put enormous effort and enthusiasm. They had been on holiday in Greece and, after being kept up all night by a delayed flight, were on their way back home to Edinburgh. Lottie was at the wheel of the car and is thought to have gone to sleep at the wheel, though no one really knows exactly what happened. Their car went into a lorry and they were both killed instantly.

Juliet said she was relieved that it was Lottie who was driving. She feels the other set of parents involved – Mark's family – had the harder role to play over this situation. Curiously, Mark had apparently always had a conviction that he would die young.

The transport police, who must all too often be the bearers of bad news in their line of duty, were quiet and considerate and did their best under the circumstances. James went back to thank them a week or so afterwards. It is a terrible job to be the first to break this kind of news to anyone. They had a cup of tea ready and it was suggested that Juliet should sit down. When she refused the tea and said she didn't want to sit, she remembers the WPC saying, 'I think you should. You're not acting normally.' They were also both determined that they must drive themselves home, despite (understandable) police pressure that they should allow themselves to be driven. 'I could not have borne to be driven by a stranger.'

They only wanted to be alone and in control, to have something – anything – to do, before shock took over completely.

Juliet says her greatest help in coping with this grievous loss has been the Leith School of Art in Edinburgh, which Lottie and Mark had opened three years before. The determination to keep this going, to staff it and raise funds for it, has been the thing that has helped her most.

Like Elizabeth Ward, James and Juliet have been able to make something positive out of their family tragedy – which is in no way to suggest it could ever be a compensation. I asked Juliet if it made grief even worse that there were no children of the marriage: she said no, it was a relief. She thinks it would have been ghastly to have to cope with small, parentless grandchildren – totally traumatic. What sort of life would the child have had? she asked. I was rather surprised about this. I suppose my own – probably more selfish – thought, was that it might have been a comfort to have a child that was part of the daughter they had lost.

Like so many other people, Juliet commented on the awful exhaustion of grief: the days when it is an effort even to move. After four years she has still not been able to cope with clearing out Lottie's clothes, or the things in her bedroom, and does not really like having to use the room for other people to sleep in but, she commented, 'there is no doubt that time does help. The pain gets less acute.'

Life continues now for this family with an outward semblance of normality, but it can never be the same again for any of them.

I asked Juliet how she would have survived the tragedy of her daughter's death if, like Susan, she had no belief in spiritual survival, and she replied, 'Unimaginably awful. I couldn't have coped.'

I thought again, as I often do, how very lucky those of us are who can take some comfort from belief in a hereafter – no matter how wavering, variable and tentative this may be – and how much I salute the courage of those who survive without this particular crutch.

Some people call belief wishful thinking.

When a married couple go through a tragedy together, one of the difficulties to be faced is that their ways of coping with the situation may be widely different. It is an over-simplification to say that women need to talk more than men. Men need to talk too, though on the whole I think they find this both harder to do and, perhaps, more difficult to admit. Certainly a husband and wife cannot always be the most effective people to comfort each other. If they are both struggling to deal, as best they can, with their own terrible loss, it is often too much to ask that they provide the right support and understanding for the other bereft partner.

In her poignant book, *Dear Isobel*, about the loss of her little daughter from a brain tumour, Georgiana Monckton touches most movingly on this difficulty, as does her husband, Piers, in the chapter he has contributed. There is a brilliant Afterword in the book by Jennie Salkeld, former Neurosurgical Liaison Sister at Great Ormond Street Hospital, which I would recommend anyone to read. I know I minded that I did not find Charlie more helpful over Amanda, and felt angry about this. I don't think I gave much, if any, thought at the time to what help he might need. I am aware that what we went through then, though it seemed awful at the time, cannot be compared to the grief of the loss of an older child, whose personality has had a chance to twine itself, like a clematis, about the tree of a family's life. Our loss was more the loss of hope than the loss of a particular and beloved person.

To the bereaved person, a loss by suicide feels like the biggest rejection of all, even if the person who committed it genuinely deluded themselves that they were doing it in the best interests of those that loved them.

One friend of mine whose husband took his own life felt he had done it because he was about to fall victim again to the terrible, black depression that had hit him once before, and that he wished to spare her from having to cope with this again. There were signs that it was coming on again, but she had not thought it was serious yet. In trying to spare her from his depression, he must already have been far too ill to realize the dreadful burden of anguish and guilt that was his legacy to her instead.

A young woman, whose husband killed himself, has spoken to me of her terror at the possibility of starting a new relationship. Some of her friends, who see this as a wonderful new beginning for her, cannot always understand the utter panic it causes her, and feel she would be self-destructive and negative if she did not seize the chance now that it has appeared.

In our life-board of Snakes and Ladders, we can cope with little snakes and little ladders but after a cataclysmic event, the tallest ladder is perhaps the most threatening of all – from this point there is such a long way to fall that it may seem preferable to lurk on one of the lower squares on the board. A window opening on to new love and possible happiness, so appealing in one way, brings with it the terrible fear of another rejection.

If you have been mortally wounded, the idea of deliberately risking hurt again can be terribly threatening.

This woman is the victim of violent mood swings, of eating problems and, with these, the extra fear of trying her friends' patience beyond endurance. She is constantly on the verge of exhaustion.

It is not always possible for those who have not experienced a life-shattering loss themselves to comprehend the many small braveries, as well as the obvious big ones, that are involved in getting back to any semblance of normal life. Attending a party, a trip to the supermarket, the initiative to make a telephone call: all these everyday things can seem infinitely threatening – let alone the huge leap towards making a new commitment to someone else.

I have also been told that after the loss of a beloved partner, especially by suicide, some people, of either sex, have gone to the other extreme and become extremely promiscuous for a time in a desperate effort to deaden their pain and try to replace something without which they feel they cannot survive. It may also be a subconscious desire for revenge – a way of punishing the dead partner for having abandoned them. Then onlookers, scenting whiffs of perceived disloyalty, can become truly censorious.

I have written of the slow puncture or the sudden burst. Another woman who told me her story, had both. Her husband had been battling against both cancer and financial losses when he took his life. Only a year later, she has covered an enormous amount of ground in terms of her own readjustment, and yet has expectations of herself that seem impossibly high to me. It is too soon to expect to be on an even keel. Time and continued understanding from friends will be her greatest allies now.

Someone whose daughter committed suicide in her twenties said sadly to me that, because of the way of her death, no one ever voluntarily mentioned this daughter to the parents any more; never brought up her name in casual conversation, or mentioned her childhood; never said things like, 'Do you remember the time when . . . ?' It was as though there was a conspiracy to negate the whole of her life, as though she had never existed. The parents, especially the mother, found this hurtful. This is a very delicate area and what will be right for one person may be disaster to another.

Another friend said to me that when tragedy overtook their family, one of her sons complained that it seemed to give all sorts of people he hardly knew the idea that they suddenly had the right to rush up and hug him. A reserved and private person, this made him cringe. I had to admit that I fear I am by nature one of these importunate, impulsive huggers!

It is impossible to guess right all the time – but I still think some response is better than no response. Better to be looked over than overlooked.

Here is a letter I was sent about the suicide of a teenage child. I have quoted it in full. I was so moved when I read it that I could hardly type it out. There is nothing I could add to this.

Grief for a child is a very poignant kind of pain, but grief for a child who has committed suicide pierces the heart with a living pain one keeps for the rest of one's life. Most people experience a sense of guilt when a loved person dies: one could have done more, been more considerate, been with them more often . . . and so on.

But parents of a child who has taken its own life 'know' that they are responsible and guilty, whatever else other people might say. So how does one cope?

For me it was a physical pain as well as in my mind. It kept sleep away for more than a year, and as there were other difficulties in my life as well, I became so weak I nearly died. In fact there was a moment when I had the chance to give up and drift away.

The pain of grief terrified me. It was like a great wave coming at me, and I fought against its approach, tightening every muscle in anticipation and knowing nothing would stop it. Gradually I learnt to relax physically and let the wave come: it was still acutely painful, but seemed to roll over me and left me exhausted, but at least passive, and I would wait quietly for the next onslaught.

When a loved person dies, family and friends and a wonderful variety of acquaintances surround one with sympathy and kindness – and it certainly helps most of us. I believe it is a mistake not to receive letters both for the bereaved and for everyone else; unexpected people have the wish to write to you, and answering the letters can fill useful hours, in empty, never-ending days. The most reassuring letters that give strength and hope, are very often from people one would not have expected to write. These letters warm the heart . . . one rarely forgets the person who wrote with sensitivity; sometimes a relationship and understanding grows between them and you which would not have flowered in normal circumstances.

It brings relief to most of us to be able to talk about one's grief with friends who share in it. However, when the death is suicidal, family and friends try to help but all are shocked out of normal relationship and there are very few words that hit the right note. One's world is upside down. How can one rethink the future – a future one no longer wants? One feels entirely alone, it is too painful to talk about it, and if one were to try, the horror is so far removed from the other person's experience, that they do not know how to respond.

Learning to live again, with 'one wing down', I feared many things that never materialized; equally I seemed incapable of anticipating hurts that could really knock me. I think I was fortunate to have been a regular churchgoer, and even more fortunate in our vicar, a dedicated Churchman, who said I was welcome to talk to him whenever I felt like it. I availed myself of this generous offer by a very busy man, and shall always be grateful for his patience, humour and tolerance.

Something that shocked me deeply was the realization that I must learn to love my surviving children . . . all the love within me seemed to have gone with H. Fortunately it soon returned, but I had not expected to experience this frightening numbing of my senses towards them.

Then one had to accept the finality of what had happened, and this was terribly painful. I had been the sort of person who thought one could always put things right. What arrogance brought down! On the positive side, I was given kindred spirits who are always there – friends who never fail. My life has not gone as planned but it has been full of interest. I am blessed to live a rural life, and the first aconite, the first snowdrop, lifts the heart, and all the followers thereafter. I can rarely grieve when I am gardening. It has become wonderful therapy, and now that I am in my sixties and see so many friends with physical restraints, I know that I am lucky.

Recently some kind person suggested I try a new therapy that was intended to soften the suffering, the pain that she knew was always within me, but the idea did not appeal. It – the hurt – is part of me now, but on rare occasions H seems to be beside me, and very briefly, I am wonderfully happy.

The writer of this letter told me that she felt she had been a very narrow person before this tragedy hit the family: the experience widened her horizons in extraordinary ways and opened her eyes to people with whom she would not otherwise have formed a friendship.

I empathize with the comment about the aconites. A friend of my mother's, who had known much trouble in her life, once said to me that after a bereavement she felt it necessary to make a conscious effort to try and recover joy in small things for however brief a moment – be it the first snowdrops, dew on a morning cobweb, the sun on one's back, or just something as simple as knowing that you feel exactly the right temperature. These are the things that have often brought me comfort.

Because I have been lucky enough to be blessed with supremely supportive family and friends, it never occurred to me to consult a professional bereavement counsellor for myself, nor do I feel now that I should have done so. However, when I started this book I decided it would be arrogant to air my personal views about grief without talking to some professionals. I also thought it would be devious to present myself for counselling without disclosing why it was that I wished to do so, so I was always open about my reasons. However, a counsellor at one organization was very unwilling to talk to me or allow me to speak to anyone else on the staff. She said I would be wasting their time. I was taken aback at this unhelpful, not to say hostile, reaction. I said mildly that I didn't think anything intended to be of help to the bereaved could be a complete waste of time, but that if it made it more acceptable, I was actually bereaved myself. She replied that after four years, and 'obviously coping perfectly well', I couldn't count myself as bereaved. Not having met me, how did she know how I was coping? I was unprepared for the effect these words had on me. I felt as if I'd been the object of an unexpected physical attack. When I put the telephone down I found myself shaking. Then I felt extremely angry. Who is to say how long grief should last?

Perhaps this was a blessing in disguise: not normally a confrontational character, it stiffened my spine enough to make me persistent, and I did eventually get to talk on the telephone to the senior counsellor of this organization. Her approach, I am happy to say, could not have been more different. This one antagonistic reaction was the exception to the rule of general helpfulness I met.

In contrast to this, another professional counsellor to whom I talked told me that her organization has clients coming for help for the first time as long as fifteen years after a bereavement. Four years into widowhood at the time of this conversation, smarting from the previous rebuff, and busy writing about death on a grey January day with a view from my window of grimy, half-thawed snow draped across the fields like dirty sheets, I found this information comforting. Perhaps I'm not doing so badly after all, I thought: I am still allowed to feel glum occasionally.

All the counsellors to whom I talked recognized patterns in grieving, though they divided it differently, some talking of four stages, some five, some even seven. The time factor or sequence may be different, some people may not experience all the emotions, but the stages do seem to be relevant to most people, and not only in connection with death but for all sorts of other losses too. It might be helpful to list some of them as put to me by one professional therapist:

Shock and denial: unable to accept the situation, or look to the future; numbness; poor memory.

Searching and pining: going back in reality or thought to past times and places; hearing keys in locks; sensing a presence; thinking, 'I must remember to tell' when it is no longer possible; poor sleep; great distress.

Anger: blaming someone – doctors, family, circumstances, fate, et cetera.

Guilt: blaming oneself: 'If only I'd . . .'; ashamed of any enjoyment.

Apathy and despair: low energy; illness; changed eating/sleeping patterns; irrational behaviour; mood swings; low self-esteem; fear of madness.

Gradual acceptance: letting go; finding new interests; new friends; looking to the future.

A common difficulty that bereavement counsellors are asked to help with is that people often think they are going mad. They need to be reassured that this is a common stage of grief and despair. A bereavement can affect a whole family, causing problems with other relationships. It is like dropping a stone into a pool: the waves and ripples spread out in wide circles. Sons or daughters may feel impelled to invite an elderly bereaved parent to come and live with them, and then be unable to cope with the stress this puts on all the family members. Older people may deeply resent giving up their independence. Husbands or wives may feel shut out by the obsession of their partner with grief for a dead child. Children may feel inadequate to compensate for a departed brother or sister. There must be many times when someone outside the immediate family circle, be it a professional or a less involved friend, can be invaluable in seeing a wider picture and helping those involved to understand other points of view and come to terms with them. One counsellor told me, 'We offer the same service, only in a more informed way, of "the holiday stranger" to whom people sometimes pour out their hearts without the fear of giving too much of themselves away to someone involved with their daily lives.'

I think one of the benefits of turning to a professional may be that most of us are terrified of boring the pants off our long-suffering friends and relations. We are conscious of having received amazing support and help, but do not want to appear insatiable. There is a pressure to recover within a certain time span, but grief does not work like this.

It is lovely to be rung up by kind well-wishers and asked how we are doing, but I have sometimes felt impelled to say that I'm fine, doing really well, and felt conscious that I am trying to give the required, and not the truthful, response, because I think that particular caller may not be able to cope with the information that at that precise moment I was actually sitting in a heap, metaphorically bleeding all over the floor: then I have heard the relief in the friend's or relation's voice because I have given them the reassurance that *they* need. Offers of comfort can be due not so much to what will help the bereaved, but what helps *us* to deal with *them*, because their pain makes us so unhappy ourselves: 'Count your blessings; look on the bright side; at least you've got such and such; don't take on so', et cetera. It is hard to face the pain of those we love.

It is only fair to admit that I have also been on the other end of this scenario, and have myself been reluctant to face the ocean of someone else's misery or self-pity, for fear it might wash over me and pull me down as well.

One woman I know – I shall call her L – seems to

me a prime example of someone who might have found professional help invaluable. She is a private person, deeply shy, who does not make close friends easily. She had a long-standing affair – a genuine love affair – with the man for whom she worked. She never had any illusion that marriage was an option. He did not want to upset his family and nor did she, nor did she wish to damage his career. No one knew about their relationship. Then he got cancer and died. L felt all her mourning had to be private so as not to hurt his wife. Not every other woman would be so altruistic. She badly needed to talk about him though, and was considering going to a bereavement counsellor, when she happened to meet one socially and heard this woman say – talking in a purely general sense – that she was strongly of the opinion that grieving should only go on for a year – an absolute maximum of two years – and thought people should always put a fixed limit on the amount of time they allowed themselves to grieve. This seemed very arbitrary to me and reminded me of Susan saying that there was a stage when she wished to recapture her raw grief as a way of keeping in touch with David. L wanted to cling on to her grief as being the only sure way she thought she would be able to feel close to her lover – the one infinitely precious person with whom she had ever had or felt she was likely to have a close relationship. Her grief was her remaining link with him and his absence left her life completely empty. This is not the same as doing a Queen Victoria over mourning and memorabilia, and refusing to meet obligations for years. L was outwardly getting on with her life, but she had no support, and no one knew how much she was bleeding inwardly.

Grief that is deeply felt, but cannot be openly acknowledged, must be terribly hard. One divorced woman told me how hard she had found it when her ex-husband – the father of her children – died. No one seemed to feel that she had a right to mourn him. She felt like a stateless person. I am thinking too of a man who had a close homosexual relationship with a married man. When his lover died, like L, he had to keep his anguish secret.

We have to make efforts to get back to normal, and it takes courage and determination to do so, but I don't think anyone else should dare to tell us how long our grief should last – you cannot simply switch it off like an oven, when a pinger rings. It seemed terribly sad that one insensitive, didactic remark, broadcast in a social situation, completely put L off seeking help.

Feelings and responses can never be an exact science.

One counsellor told me she thought one thing that should not be said to anyone facing a loss is, 'I know just how you feel.' We none of us know that. We can take an imaginative leap and say we can guess – or think we can – how *we* should feel. I thought this was an interesting point, and know I have been guilty of using those words myself. It is easy to fall into the trap of telling people about our own bereavements in an effort to show understanding, when the only helpful course of action is to listen – really listen – to what they need to say about their own feelings. She raised the point that men find it much harder to find help from their own sex when they are bereaved than women.

Jenni, who was widowed after her husband's long fight against leukaemia, is an ordained priest. She was shaken to discover how uneasy many of her male colleagues were with her bereaved state. 'They might well have been helpful if I'd made an appointment and gone to consult them in their professional capacity, but they couldn't cope with me in an everyday setting. At a conference I had to attend soon after R's death, my fellow clergy were far worse at knowing how to react to me than my lay friends.' Her parishioners were a huge help, however. She found it difficult when people said to her that she was 'lucky to have her faith'. 'What faith?' she felt like answering in her first anguish. Like Diana Hare and me, she found the suggestion of luck in those circumstances unhelpful. God seemed distant. Later she said this gave her new insights into the words, 'My God, my God why hast thou forsaken me?' Jenni, who adored her husband, found the feeling of separation from him, when he seemed to withdraw from her because all his energies were going into fighting his illness, specially hard to bear. Like me, she lost her mother within two years of becoming a widow, and found this double loss very hard. I am sure Jenni will be able to give very special ministry to the bereaved.

Many priests are wonderful at the time of the funeral and during the first week, but the 'after-care' can be minimal or non-existent, as Jane noticed after the cot death of Freddie in the letter quoted at the beginning of this book. I have to say, I think that in her case this was a terrible omission on the part of any priest. Of course, this is not always so. Another friend of mine who had been a card-carrying atheist at the time of a major bereavement received such loving and continuing support from her vicar and local church that she is now a deeply committed Christian herself.

There are many losses apart from death. 'You are lucky to be a widow,' one woman said to me. Her husband of thirty years had traded her in for a newer model. 'At least you were left with your self-esteem intact.' Food for thought. Something as final as death can be more straightforward to cope with: there are no continuing choices.

'You do not have to have a body to have a bereavement,' someone said to a friend of mine, speaking of Alzheimer's disease, that terrible stealer of personality while the physical body goes on, and I remembered my mother-in-law. Journalist David Morgan Rees has given me permission to quote his moving poem about this subject:

The Visit

'I'm *not* your darling,' she says with vehemence
When I greet her lovingly.
My mother's face is pinched,
Her voice shrill and agitated.
She does not recognize me as her son.

I cannot reconcile my love with this denial
Though I know her mind's shadowed vagaries
As she moved through her ninety years.
She sits in her room and stares
With anger at my intrusion.

Then she grows calmer, her face softens
Into the beauty that is her gift
To memories of happier, younger days.
But still the lack of recognition hurts.

She talks of me as if I'm absent.
'Where's my son? When will he come?'
I try to establish my identity
But my credentials do not pass the test.
I hold my photo next to my face
And there is a momentary flicker.
Then it's gone and the question repeated.

I feel guilty, as if an imposter
Sitting in her room, trying to impress.
We make disjointed conversation.
I give her a dutiful allowance of my time.
As I leave I kiss her goodbye.

She accepts this with a sudden smile.
'Take care,' she says. 'Please come again.'
Am I at last accepted as her son
Or am I still the unknown visitor?

David Morgan Rees 1996

The loss of health, as Charlie and I learnt, is a grievous one.
We can mourn for the loss of part of our body in an operation
– the loss of a limb, for instance – and meet with just the
same awkwardness and panic that a few people show to those
bereaved by death. A friend of ours, who lost both his legs
in the war as a very young man, remembers the difficulty
some of his friends had when they first met him again. When
he said, 'Nice to see you again' to a down-to-earth Yorkshire

farmer, the answer was an unembarrassed, 'Better you'd never gone away!' By contrast when he went, in the wheelchair he then used, to a British Legion meeting, friends who had known him all his life 'looked steadfastly at the ceiling – anywhere but at me!' I asked this friend whether he is legless in his dreams. Not one to indulge in introspection or brood on his difficulties, typically he had never thought about it. But when asked by me to try, he made the discovery that after fifty years, in his dreams he still has both legs. I thought this was fascinating.

I have been asked to mention in this book what my own faith is and – panic! – how I pray, two subjects I had intended to duck. However, for what it is worth, I will try.

I do have a faith, pliable I hope rather than rigid, though quite strong, but I am frightened of defining it too closely. The moment I write something about my beliefs it seems immediately either half true or half untrue, anyway dauntingly inadequate. I am not keen to put salt on the tail of this particular bird. All the same, it is important to me.

Since I was a very small child I have had a strong sense of something 'other' – a something that coexists both near us and within us, and can sometimes be glimpsed or felt, but which is usually just out of sight or out of reach. Perhaps I should admit that I do occasionally, always unexpectedly, see or hear 'ghosts', for want of a better word. Whether such experiences will one day be explained as being like photographs on the atmosphere, I don't know. Charlie and I once saw a ghost together – a woman who walked across and through the bonnet of our car as we were driving. It gave us a serious fright because we thought we'd hit her, and it was only as we watched her impossibly going on walking away that we realized that she was in the dress of several centuries ago. This sort of sighting is not what I mean when I talk about something 'other', and I have occasionally had experience of actual 'presences' – rather than just random sightings – too.

I was brought up in the Church of England, and still attend my local church, not every Sunday, but quite often. I suppose I find the services (well, some of them) like a comfortable old shoe, though old shoes are getting harder to come by now. I am not at all against new forms of worship, which can give us fresh insights and be rejuvenating, but I think it would be sad indeed if we ceased to value and use a rich heritage.

I have problems with organized religion, and am not a good team player. I find both joining and belonging difficult – but I also think it is arrogant to think I can go it alone. I adore church music, love the old words of the Bible and the *Book of Common Prayer*, which I use and take comfort from, but I would no longer define myself as belonging exclusively to any particular denomination. I find the idea of any denomination – or religion – being exclusive very troubling.

I have doubts as well as faith. They are uncomfortable to live with, but I think doubts are valuable. It is certainties that usually start wars.

Some of the best spiritual teaching I have received was on the traditionally Christian island of Iona (where the veil between one world and the next always seems a little thinner) by a Tibetan Buddhist lama who teaches at Dharmsala and works for the Dalai Lama. His approach, that if we found any value in his teaching, we should first try to adapt it to the faith in which we had been brought up, seemed wonderfully

refreshing, and a contrast to the converting zeal of funda-
mentalism, which, from whatever quarter it comes, sends me
running in the opposite direction.

I like the idea that we should seek to encounter and
learn from 'other men of faith' – a better way of putting it
than 'men from another faith'. God, again for want of any
other word, must be greater than any of the tight little boxes
in which man, used in the generic not the gender sense, tries
to confine such a power. (I hate the word 'person'. I think we're
getting very silly about our terminology.) I have memories of
this remarkable teacher, Gen Rinpoche, temporarily tooth-
less after a much-needed visit to a British dentist, a woolly
hat he'd purchased in Oban warming his bald head, striding
about the grey Hebridean rocks in his saffron and magenta
robes. It was like sighting a bird of paradise where one
expected to see a sandpiper. An immensely humorous as well
as humane man, he was often laughing. It makes me think
what a pity it is that we don't get more sermons about the
wit and humour of Jesus, who must have been stunningly
good company.

I don't consider myself good at prayer, though I do try. I
have attempted to learn various meditative and contemplative
techniques, but my own lack of self-discipline is always a
stumbling block. I like to chat away to God, Don Camillo
style, and think it is a pity if we are brought up to make
prayers into a sort of shopping list, rather than a lovely
telephone call about nothing in particular – an attempt to
communicate with the Divine. As with people, I suspect
listening is probably more important than speaking. I have
a mental vision of the switchboard angels, tearing their wings
over all the requests which block the lines, when they are
longing to get us to take an incoming call. On the whole I

now try, not very successfully, to avoid praying for particular outcomes – with one exception. I think prayers for help, for other people or ourselves, are often answered, though seldom in the way we expect. I have looked up the lovely word 'grace' in my dictionary. There are many definitions, including 'a free and unmerited favour of God towards man', and 'divine assistance and power'. Surely we can ask for that? When asked to pray for anyone, I find the conception of 'holding someone in the light' helpful. Visualization is becoming a well-recognized tool in fighting illness now. It is, for me, a way of praying that I find possible, and I fall back on a favourite quotation. I think it's by the healer Dorothy Kerrin, though I'm not sure about this. 'There is no more powerful ray than a thought sent out in love.' I love that.

I wish I had known about these ideas during the bad patch of my early married years. I remember vividly sitting in the Hammersmith Hospital beside the dying Val and thinking, 'How can I pray for her to get better when I know she's going to die?' Perhaps I could have prayed for grace, for us both, and left it at that.

When we are in great trouble, I think prayer is often beyond us, and that is the time when other people should do it for us. It is interesting that in a 'blind' experiment in America, a survey on heart-surgery patients showed marked benefits among those that were being prayed for – but didn't know it.

Charlie and I were constantly amazed by each other's different kinds of mind. We often disagreed. 'What are you thinking?' he would sometimes ask me, and always thought my answers most peculiar. He said it was weird to live with, and be so close to, someone who had such curious ideas churning round their head. When I asked him the same question he would often say, 'Nothing.' 'Oh, come on,' I would goad him. 'You must be thinking of *something*.'

Then he might admit that he was counting: raspberries if he was picking them; daffodil bulbs if he was planting them; music if he was playing the piano or organ; and, latterly, stitches when he sewed. He said it helped to make his mind a blank. This used to infuriate me until it occurred to me that, while I rushed off on silent retreats ('All that frightful introspection,' said Charlie) or went to Hebridean islands to listen to esoteric teaching and tried to learn to meditate, Charlie, at home, was achieving naturally under his rhododendron bush or stitching at his needlepoint, exactly what I was trying to learn so unsuccessfully elsewhere. It was a humbling idea. He pooh-poohed it when I bowled this new thought at him, but he looked rather smug all the same.

One of the reasons I think he made so many remarkable recoveries, apart from his strong fighting spirit, was his ability to concentrate on and, better still, enjoy whatever he was doing. If he was listening to music, then he was absorbed in the music, if he gardened, then the garden filled his being. He had a great ability to enjoy, to the full, a good moment while it lasted. He certainly wasn't dwelling on his illness or himself.

I'm more like a dog let out in a field with lots of lovely early morning smells, dashing about on one burning scent after another. I flit from thought to thought.

I think life must have a purpose, however darkly veiled this may be to us now. I accept that much of life is a mystery, and personally feel it is a mistake to try to pretend otherwise. However much we may *believe*, as I do, in an afterlife we cannot *know* for certain, nor do I think we are meant to do so. Therefore, I suppose I have to call myself agnostic. If we are honest, aren't we all agnostic? While I accept with my mind that I cannot know the answers, I wish I could feel as confident as a priest I knew who always said, 'I can't *know*, but I *believe* – but I would stake my life on that belief.' I would love to say the same, but knowing my own limitations I wouldn't like to bet on it. I guess that we're just meant to do the best we can with whatever is under our noses.

The idea of karma or progress of the spirit – or, of course, lack of progress, a retaking of A levels as it were – is quite attractive to me, and I think some sort of reincarnation might be a possibility. It's one of the few ideas that makes a sort of sense out of chaos. It was quite a widely accepted idea in the time of Christ ('Who think ye that I am?') though perhaps it has always been more easily acceptable to Eastern rather than Western Christianity. Certainly Origen (185–254), the great Eastern theologian of the early Church, believed in it, and I know many Christians of all denominations who accept it, even if it is not the official teaching of their particular branch of the Church.

I have a distrust of labels, and of having faith, or anything else, put into tight little preconceived pigeon-holes – and I certainly have no wish to force my tentative ideas on anyone else.

I belong to a network of fellow searchers, which gathers on Iona each spring. Few of us manage to go every year, but we have strong bonds with each other. We number among us several Roman Catholics, Baptists, representatives of the Churches of England and Scotland, Sufis, Buddhists and a Japanese Quaker, to mention but a few. Some of us don't hang our hats on any particular peg. We resist giving ourselves a name, or having any particular definition. Years ago my son christened us the Crusties – Cranky Upwardly

Spiritual Triers. I like the idea – much more fun than being Yuppies. On one occasion when some of the group were attempting a dance meditation in the early morning on Iona – a wildly funny spectacle when performed in waterproofs, sou'westers and boots in driving Scottish rain – a disapproving but fascinated onlooker came and asked suspiciously, 'Are you Druids?' 'No, we're Fluids,' one of our group brilliantly replied.

I think dreams can be a useful way of accessing the inner wisdom that we have locked up inside us. In the months following Charlie's death I had endless dreams that were variations on the theme of rebuilding walls. In these dreams I always had a choice. I have a friend who is a dream analyst, and have heard her give some fascinating interpretations of people's dreams, but it didn't need anyone very specialized to tell me that this was about the choice to rebuild my life. Once or twice in my life I have had some really important 'teacher dreams' that have had a profound effect on me.

Sometimes I dream about Charlie himself, but not very often now. It seems to go in phases. Very occasionally he is there in a dream, as he was once always there in the background of my life, though not necessarily taking an active part in whatever is going on. Then I wake and briefly assume he is still beside me. The moment of realization that this is no longer so is always desolate.

Someone once said to me that children are far more comfortable with the inexplicable than adults are, and that to most children it is quite acceptable to say, 'I don't know. It is a mystery.' I find that acceptable too. I don't know about arrivals, but I think that the journey itself is important, and that on a spiritual one it is just as good to travel hopefully as on any other kind of journey – and much more fun.

My views may not be entirely orthodox but, neverthe-less, in times of trouble I do turn to prayer, I have found my faith a comfort, and I do feel strongly that human death is not the end for the individual soul. Perhaps it is a question of vibrating on a different level. I hope I pray in good times as well as in times of desperation. It seems to me as important to make prayers of joy as well as prayers of woe, prayers of gratitude as well as those of supplication. If I had to try and produce one 'Desert Island' prayer it would be the much-loved prayer of St Francis: 'Lord make me an instru-ment of your peace.' I carry a copy of this prayer in my wallet, always. They are the words I fall back on when all others fail.

I started my story with my first memory of laughter. I should like to end it with a quotation from Callisthenes:

'Laughter is man's declaration of freedom. It is his refusal to go into bondage to his troubles.' Perhaps it is the thing that has helped me most of all to get through times of darkness and despair.

I have found this book extremely difficult to write. Sometimes I have felt I was drowning in it; often I have felt I was mad to attempt it.

Now I am finding it impossible to finish. I am terribly aware of its inadequacies, of my inability to express what I would like to convey; of all the many omissions there are. In a way it is a book that can never be finished. If, as a sharing and a joining of hands, any of it is helpful to other people who are facing or coping with loss, then I shall feel privileged, and it will have been worth it.

I offer it to all who are bereaved – in whatever way – with love.

Gateways

Some people seek
a sacred place to pray,
or meditate, legs crossed
eyes shuttered, spirits far away,
touching tranquillity
with upturned palms

– but others like
to lean upon a gate
and let the sun's arm
rest across their backs;

watch circus swallows,
skimming farmyard stacks,
meticulously time
their aerobatic skills
– while shadows murmur mantras
on far hills.

Long green diminuendos then
fluted by secret willow-wrens
shall be a bell, an Evensong – a psalm.

To each their individual
source of calm.

Further Reading

Susan Hill, *In the Springtime of the Year* (Penguin, 1977).

Susan Hill, *Family* (Penguin, 1990).

Caryle Hirshberg and Marc Ian Barasch, *Remarkable Recovery: What Extraordinary Healings Can Teach Us About Getting Well and Staying Well* (Headline, 1995).

Patricia Kelley and Maggie Callanan, *Final Gifts: Understanding and Helping the Dying* (Hodder and Stoughton, 1992).

Elisabeth Kübler-Ross, *On Death and Dying* (Routledge, 1990).

Elisabeth Kübler-Ross, *On Children and Death* (Collier Paperbacks, 1993).

C. S. Lewis, *A Grief Observed* (Faber and Faber, 1966).

D. Manning, *Don't Take My Grief Away: What to do When You Lose a Loved One* (Harper and Row, 1984).

Georgiana Monckton with Hilary Burden, *Dear Isobel* (Vermilion, 1994).

Dr Melvin Morse and Paul Perry, *Closer to the Light: Learning from Children's Near-death Experiences* (Souvenir Press, 1991).

Ned Sherrin (ed.), *Remembrance: An Anthology of Readings, Prayers and Music Chosen for Memorial Services* (Michael Joseph, 1996).

Jill Truman, *Letter to My Husband* (Hodder and Stoughton, 1988).

Allegra Taylor, *Acquainted with the Night: A Year on the Frontiers of Death* (Fontana, 1989).

Elizabeth Ward, *Timbo: A Struggle for Survival* (Sidgwick and Jackson, 1986).

Agnes Whitaker (ed.), *All in the End is Harvest: An Anthology for Those Who Grieve* (Cruse, 1987).

Useful Addresses and Telephone Numbers

The British Kidney Patient Association
Bordon
Hampshire
GU35 9JZ
Tel 01420 472021

The Child Bereavement Trust
Harleyford Estate
Henley Road
Marlowe
Buckinghamshire
(NB This is not a direct counselling service)

Child Death Helpline
Tel 0171 829 8685
(10.00am–1.00pm Monday, Wednesday and Friday
7.00pm–10.00pm every evening)

The Compassionate Friends
53 North Street
Bristol
BS3 1EN
Tel 0117 953 9639

CRUSE Bereavement Care
126 Sheen Road
Richmond
Surrey
TW9 1UR
Tel 0181 940 4818

CRUSE Bereavement Helpline: 0181 332 7227
(Monday to Friday 9.30am–5.00pm)
CRUSE Youth Line: 0181 940 3131
(Friday 5.00pm–9.00pm and Saturday 11.00am–6.00pm)

Hospice Information Service
St Christopher's Hospice
51 Lawrie Park Road
London
SE26 6DZ
Tel 0181 778 9252

National Association of Bereavement Services
20 Norton Folgate
London
E1 6DB
Tel 0171 247 1080

SANDS, the Stillbirth and Neonatal Death Society
Tel 0171 436 5881